Cairn-Space

Cairn-Space

*Poems, Prayers, and Mindful Amblings about the Places
We Set Aside for Meaning, Prayer, and the Sacramental
Life in the New Monasticism*

N. Thomas Johnson-Medland, CSJ, OSL

RESOURCE *Publications* · Eugene, Oregon

CAIRN-SPACE
Poems, Prayers, and Mindful Amblings about the Places We Set Aside for Meaning,
Prayer, and the Sacramental Life in the New Monasticism

Resource Publications
An Imprint of Wipf and Stock Publishers
199 W. 8th Ave., Suite 3
Eugene, OR 97401
www.wipfandstock.com

ISBN 13: 978-1-60899-683-4

Manufactured in the U.S.A.

This book is dedicated to Zoe; the one who took my heart, filled it, and gave it back to me. I await you, in glory, with joy.

"A brother in Scetis went to ask for a word from Abba Moses and the old man said to him, 'Go and sit in your cell and your cell will teach you everything.'"

—The Sayings of the Desert Fathers

Abba Anthony said: "The time is coming when people will be seized by manias and will behave like madmen. And if they see anyone acting reasonably, they will rise up against him saying: 'You are insane.' And they will have accurately said this to him, for he will not be like them."

—The Sayings of the Desert Fathers

"Opposed to the idea that the world of perception is the bottom of reality, the mystics plunge into what is beneath the perceptible. What they attain in their quest is more than a vague impression or spotty knowledge of the imperceptible. 'Penetrating to the real essence of wisdom . . . they are resplendent with the radiance of supernal wisdom (Zohar II).' Their eyes perceive things of this world, while their hearts reverberate to the throbbing of the hidden."

—Rabbi Abraham Joshua Heschel
The Mystical Element in Judaism

Contents

Introduction

CAIRNS HAVE DECORATED THE landscapes of cultures throughout time. Piles of stone—one stone placed on top of another—are set in place all over the earth to recall battles, identify burial sites, mark trails, and spur hearts and minds to remember sacred, noble, and critical events. They are landmarks. They are sacramental presences in space and time.

I first encountered cairns in my spiritual journey while staying at retreat houses on the East Coast. Most of the cairns were built in out of the way places along trails. Folks who had gone on retreat had constructed the rock piles where they had had spiritual experiences of "metanoia" or conversion of heart. Since that day I have seen them in countless locations, but mostly while hiking or on retreat. They are outward manifestations of peoples' inner realities.

Part of the beauty of cairns is their impermanence. You need to restructure them periodically—to interact with them and share some sort of relationship—as they fall down or apart with the passage of time and the weather of our days on this earth-place. Rock slides off of rock and needs to be replaced. Rain erodes the supportive earth beneath cairns and more dirt needs to be added if the rocks are to stay above the ground. People automatically reach for the stones, to rebuild the piles, to shift the dirt when they see them dismantled or in disarray. Cairns help people work things out.

It is the same with our spiritual lives. We are constantly building our lives in God. We develop individual practices in our spiritual lives and we have beliefs, hopes, dreams, and memories. They are the cairns that dot the landscape of our lives: of our heart, and mind, and soul. Each practice is made up of many parts; as are the beliefs, hopes, dreams, and memories. These are the stones; piled on stones.

Scripture is a cairn. Prayer is a cairn. Worship is a cairn. Icons are cairns. Mind is a cairn. Emotion is a cairn. Community itself is a cairn.

All matter and manifest phenomenon are cairns of something. Everything stands sacramentally as an indicator of something else. Mind and matter reflect things beyond themselves and unfold panoplies of dimension with each encounter. One thing leads us to another, as the intrinsic holographic nature of reality is exposed—woven in and through everything that is.

Some days the cairns fall apart. Some days they are steady and true. Sometimes we can pass them by using them as grid-markers on our travels. Sometimes we must stop and take the time to re-establish what they stand to represent.

We are always about the process of building and rebuilding our lives and the cairns in them—whether they are solid markers on the outside of our lives or are ethereal markers on the inside of our lives. Things don't always hold together. Memories are just as fragile as stone piles standing against the elements. Meaning falls apart—apparently. This speaks to our fragility and the frailty of life itself.

Cairns speak to the frailty of all matter and of the mind-stuff contained throughout that matter. Meaning often needs to be reinvested in things. Special signs and markers along the trail of life must often be rearranged so we can carry their presence into the future. Things get disturbed and out of place.

All of the things that are markers in our lives are opportunities to go inside ourselves, discover meaning; and in that meaning, uncover God. There are special dates in our lives: baptisms, confirmations, graduations, new jobs, marriages, and deaths. Each of these are cairns to us—calling out to us even though the day of their happening has passed. There are special people in our lives; special places, too. These are also cairns. These are outward manifestations of inward realities that change us, and shape us, and inform every molecule of our existence. These milestones of life are far from gone, they are woven into our consciousness in a way that often seems elusive, but they are present and often are the "hidden cause" of the direction and hope our journey assumes.

Cairns like all markers are meant to remind us of something. That remembrance is calling us to come, sit, review, and re-connect. They sign for us to go inside and link-up with an event, a process, a person, or an idea. They ask us to wrestle with things we may have tucked away— just out of memory. This wrestling is a form of relating to the things we are remembering. They are episodes in meaning. Things do matter; they tell us something. Everything has meaning.

Cairns reveal and engender a wrestling process in our lives. They show us how we assign meaning and power to what we have seen, tasted, heard, sensed, smelled, and handled with our own hands—with our own lives.

Because they straddle meaning, cairns are sacramental. They are outward manifestations of inward realities; that is, things on the outside that reveal what is important to us, and how things seem to work on the inside—behind the veil of the visible.

In the true mystic tradition, everything straddles meaning and is potentially available to reveal the inner life, God Himself, and all that Is. Everything around us and within us is a cairn toward the experience of the inner life, God Himself, and all that Is.

Everything is a sacramental cairn if we are watchful, attentive, and open to its presence and what it reveals. Phenomenon have meaning beyond themselves. Meaning unfolds when we intentionally create a place to watch it blossom.

In the wrestling of remembrance, we bring the meaning of our memories to the fore and we dust it off. We stand before all phenomenal reality and wrap ourselves around and all through existence, perception, conception, and being; and then we store that in consciousness.

We encounter things anew because of cairns. They are visible stories from our days gone by; stories that ask us to somehow interact with those past moments and create new moments of growth right here in the present; bringing what was into what is. Simple things reveal eternity.

I am encouraged by the sight of familiar cairns around the camp where we now live. They instantly bring back memories of my past that bolster me up and remind me of who I am and who I have been. I may have added a stone to a pile because I sat and prayed at this place. I may have added a stone because I sang a hymn in this spot. I may have built a cairn to mark off the place of my repentance. I may have laid a cairn to remind me Jesus spoke to me here. Cairns shape who I am becoming using the stuff of who I have been.

Cairns lead us somewhere. They lead us to and provide us with a sacred space— to a particular spot here on this earth-place or within our interior-space. From within this spot we recreate sacred time anew. They ask us to stop. They ask us to pause and recall—taking a moment to get our bearings.

It is not uncommon to find stone cairns that have been set up as trail markers. These geologic GPS coordinates, piled on the ground, help us to find our way. We remember our way in life because of the piles all around us.

The photo albums that lay about our home are GPS co-ordinates to other places in time and space. Each picture, a cairn that marks whole chapters of life that have seemingly disappeared. The birth of our sons, the hiking of a trail, a trip to the Isle of Skye; they are not gone. The photos remind me of the place in my consciousness within which I have planted those days and ways of life. As I water the seeds of my past, I am informed with a whole new vigor that my life has led me to this moment. This moment is built on so much more than I can see; but it is available within me.

We are called to pull the past into the present in order to shape our future—in our remembering. This is always the power of signs. They lead us to our future, by way of our past. We stand at a cairn and remember; we dream, we hope, we become.

This is not unlike the call of Jesus to "do this in memory of me"; to celebrate the Eucharist. The cairns in this Jesus-meeting are the species of bread and wine. They bring clarity to this moment and present us with images and facts that may not be visible, but live deeply in us as realities we assent to. We learn that we are to be broken and poured out for the life of the world as these Jesus-meeting cairns suggest. The words "in memory" or "in remembrance" of Jesus in this short passage come from the Greek word "anamnesis." This word is all about the concept of bringing the past into the present and the present into the past. It is a merging or confluence of time.

The cairns we speak of from this time forward will be cairns that may embody all of this. They may mark off God-space, heart-space, memories, or ideas. They may reveal hidden causes in the fabric of our phenomenology, or hint for us to listen for the whispering wind; sacramental cairns on the landscape of our lives. They may point to interior dimensions we had no idea existed within our heart, and mind, and soul. We will amble around the ideas of sacred-space, prayer-space, and sacramental living. We will encounter and wrestle with God all along the way. We will look for and stop at the cairns along the geography of our spiritual heritage.

What markers have we used to remember God in prayer? What markers have we laid to remind us that union is possible? How has the Church (itself a cairn of God) found its way and marked its journey on this earth-place? What have we learned from all that we have lived? Who has been important to us? What have they revealed in the way of meaning?

Jacob erected a cairn after he awoke from his dream. He piled stones on top of the stone he had rested his head on through the night. An odd pillow for some. His dream was of a ladder reaching from heaven to earth. In that dream there were angels ascending and descending on the ladder. Jacob marked that place of "holy encounter" and named it Beth-El; the "Place of God." It later became the place of meeting in the Temple of Israel—the Holy of Holies. His proclamation that "surely God has been in this place" is a critical passage in understanding the meaning of cairns in our lives. They mark off epiphanies and theophanies: God-meeting places.

Cairns are not meant to be towers of Babel, reaching to the heavens to find God—somehow off in the future. They are meant to wake us up to finding God right here—NOW—right among us. We encounter a cairn, we stop, and we turn within to figure out the meaning behind the encounter that is marked off by these rocks. What does this place mean? What does it exude? What does it call us into ourselves to find? This is how it is with everything there is. Everything has the chance to be a marker of union with the Divine—NOW. Not off in the future. Not if we do "just one more thing, or build it just a bit higher." HERE. NOW.

I am sure Babel must have started as a cairn, but the obsession of the task carried the builders away. They forgot they were laying a marker and figured they could keep building a stairway to heaven. Out of control, and perhaps believing "more is better", they thought they could navigate the heavens by building an escalator to God. They got lost in their project. The true stairway was within.

Babel shows us the natural outcome of trying to build a cairn high enough to experience the abode of God outside of our heart. Once we reach a certain fevered pitch, and the rocks are high enough, we forget that God is accessible within and our ability to communicate becomes hampered. Trying to climb to God on rocks, our language is put to confusion. We begin to lose our ability to make sense and interpret all that we see. Babel is a cairn gone bad.

It reminds me of the present nature of the Church. Our lives in Christ were meant to be a testimony of God with us, God within us. We started building and then lost control. We built the pile so big that confusion descended on us and everything went to pieces. Mainline denominations are failing because—like Babel—we have focused on building "the machine." We thought our tower would take us to God; that our buildings and our programs would take us to God. Again, the stairway is within. The heart is the sacred space, not the program, or the building, or the tower.

Cairns are simple rock piles on the surface of the earth, marking spaces in which we encountered and wrestled with God in the common-place hugger-mugger of our daily existence. They are meant to help us remember our dreams and meetings and to use those memories to live our lives more fully into the future. Cairns are asterisks on the landscape and geography of our simple lives. But, they are powerful asterisks. Like all images, they will fade and breakdown; our analogies will sometimes fail. But, as markers and asterisks, they are starting points. If one does not begin somewhere, one has not begun.

THESE SIMPLE FOODS

Holding
these simple foods,
bread
and wine,
I am forced into
my heart
to meet Jesus,
to wrestle with Him
as He changes me
into body
and blood.
This remembrance
is so real,
I am undone
and become someone I would

not have become
if we did not
meet
to eat
His sacrifice.
They
mark more than
time along the
way of my life.
They
mark time
along the
path of God with
man.
Simple
foods are they
which bring the
heavens down
to the earth
and raise our dirt
to the cosmos
above.
With these gifts –
given and returned –
we become terrestrial angels
and celestial men.
One space
one time
for all places
and through all time.

As humans we are always processing the world around us. We bring it inside of us, encounter it, wrestle with it, become transformed by it, and live our lives based on these adjustments—these transformations. Our lives are changed by these meetings.

In essence, everything in our lives is a cairn of meaning. Everything around us means something to us. Everything around us informs us and moves us into some sort of transformative encounter.

We store all that we encounter in a consciousness that eludes us. The mystery of what things mean is inside of us. Because of that the mystic heart knows that everything exists on the edge of becoming a sacrament. It all rides on the decision of the will.

The meaning of things in our lives changes the world around us as we affect the rest of life with the identity we become in the process. People help us to become new people. Places enable us to adjust how we live. Objects transform our present into future. Old things pass away and all things become new. These meetings are themselves markers of who we have been over time: elements of our own presence.

We leave markers everywhere. We tend to remember those that are in the places we have had our wrestling-encounters. These larger events in life are easier to remember. We save the memories of places where something special and memorable occurred. Some of these markers are left in the outside world as mementos, cairns, gardens, chapels, and grottoes. Some of these markers are left in the inside world as impressions, feelings, thoughts, dreams, and hopes; pieces of our becoming. Whether they are outside or inside, these markers are our cairns. That they may be outside or inside moves them into sacramental reality.

"How Great Thou Art" is a cairn for me. Inside the meaning of this marker along the way is a heart and mind filled with wonder, connections, and grandparents. I loved this hymn—and still do—because of its importance to my maternal grandmother. Mom-mom loved that hymn. Mom-mom loved that hymn because her mother loved that hymn. I sang it with abandon in her memory at church each Sunday it was selected, and again at my grandfather's funeral. It became a family cairn over time.

Mom-mom and Pop-pop became real to me as I sang each note. They became real in my heart. Every time I sang it, a neural pathway was wired from my insides to God and to my grandparents. When I sang it, I became one with God, with myself, and with my grandparents. It was a hyperlink to multiple sites. It became a communication of great import. I stored this memory inside for future visits of and to the hymn.

The time we have shared together on this earth-space is littered with markers of our lives together. My sons are cairns for me. I can look at them and remember the various stages and "people they have been." When they were little, they said things I will carry inside for the rest of my life. Things that made me laugh, or cry. Their concerts, their plays and pageants, the camping trips and vacations; these things mark time for me.

Their presence in my life helps me to rebuild who I am on a daily basis. Sometimes a simple smile can take me back over years and places. All of our cairns have the potential of doing this. Everything can be a trip wire for being snared in meaning.

All of the places we build and set aside for prayer and remembrance are simply the "subconscious mind" making signposts leading us inside. All that we have been in the past leaves a trail of breadcrumbs for us to find along the way. We stumble on the crumbs, pick them up, and remember the value and meaning we were a part of at some other time. We follow this communion trail into our own selves. What we find is a consciousness littered with moments and meaning; a matrix of all that has gone on before. We find a space within that provides us with the opportunity to sit and taste the morsels we have collected along the way.

If we look at all of the things we hold as dear, we will see our cairns; we will see the trail of breadcrumbs that leads us in. If we notice all of the places we have been transformed and changed, we will see our cairns. If we recognize the high points and low points of our lives, we will see our cairns. If we remember all of those people who have reached out to us throughout our lives, we will see our cairns. If we note each book, thought, notion, and idea we have fleetingly held, we will see our cairns. If we were able to unpack the events of each breath of our lives, we would see our cairns—all of them.

If we follow the lead and meaning these cairns provide, we are blessed to be able to find an interior room—a space inside ourselves—in which to settle down and remember. We can trace the memory into a quiet chamber of the heart and hold it in our grasp there; gently realizing its depth. If we cannot immediately find a shelter within, these cairns require us to search hard until we find one, or to build one ourselves.

And so, we find or build a chapel, a cell, or a cave in our heart where we may sit and unpack the meaning of our lives. We build on this space, to sit and sup with the Divine One who is the ground of all being.

We commune with God and all that we have been and all that we have become. We bring into the tabernacle of our heart the fullness of our mind and soul.

We have this place in us—whether we recognize it or not—that is our TRUE SELF; a place where we hold all of the strings of the awareness of our life. It is the place where all things come together. It is the place where God dwells. We retreat there in time of trouble and change. This place is called the heart. This cairn-space is a dot in eternity; a spiritual atom within which all creation is born and housed.

If we can recognize this process of going within and find this place that is within, we will be on the right road. We will be living up to our full potential as sacramental beings. We will have struck out on the most sacred journey—the journey to the heart—and we will have found there not only a home, but our true selves. In fact, the heart is the greatest cairn there is. It is the cairn established by God, to mark off our experiences of His Presence. The heart is the Holy of Holies.

This is just another way of looking at what is inside of us. The Fathers of the Church called this the Royal Road. The Royal Road always leads us to the place where God dwells in us. It leads us to the heart.

There is a longing deep within us; a yearning for this heart space within which we find oneness. It is the place we find our core identity. We await opportunities to settle into our being and feel a unity with God and all that is a part of His creation. Every experience of worship is a longing that we might discover the Presence of God in our lives and yield to that Presence. We perform acts of kindness with the hopes of catching a glimpse of God in the beggars and sick. We look for signs outside of what we sense inside.

Our eyes dart this way and that looking for a place we can call our own, a place of meeting. We want to meet the Divine One and do it again and again. We search desperately for cairns and markers that will call us into this place. We even try to buy and consume things that we believe will help us achieve this goal of "inwardness." This place exists already. We buy books that give us clues. We attend workshops that reveal the way. We must simply interpret the cairns along the way as signs that point in.

Setting out and finding God-spaces, meeting-places, and realms of connection is really what "the path" is all about. Some people recognize that this quest for unity and relationship is at the root of everything we do—NOW. Finding God drives us to search all the more. The markers on the outside help move us to the inside, and there we wait for Godot. And, although this space exists in all of us, it is paradoxically waiting to be built.

Some tell us that waiting for Godot or searching for God is an empty task; it is absurd. But, it is not the search for the Holy One (the search for our core self and its relation to God) that is empty and absurd in the end. What is empty and absurd is not recognizing that we are all seeking wholeness in God—NOW.

We all hunger and thirst to find our completion in the Divine Wholeness. Some pretend they are looking for something other than God. They believe they aspire to be "better" people or more "learned." It is simply that they do not know to call this aching passion within a hungering for God and the divine completion this represents. They have not examined the lineaments of this craving. All craving for completeness is a craving for the Holy One. It is a yearning to be One with the One. It is the rest of Saint Augustine that is only put to rest when it rests in God.

This path of hungering, longing, craving, and desiring is a path toward the heart. The heart is the place of ultimate encounter and union. Whether we believe we are questing for wholeness, integrity, actualization, or God, the quest is the same. In the non-Christian East it is said that we already have all that we long for; we must simply wake up.

We are hunting the Divine. We look everywhere for the perfect spot to unite. We turn everything upside-down to find our center—our heart. We look all around outside, to find the place that is inside. The greatest cairn is already within, and at the same time it clambers to be established. We have what we need, we must simply wake up.

Ultimately, all cairns are about getting into heart-space and experiencing the relationship we have with the Creative Father. Each cairn asks us to look at Him through the lens of some idea, topic, or event. "What does this marker say about who we are and where we have been with Him?" Everything has the ability to make us hungry for union with God—NOW.

When we find the cairns or our life, we must sit with them and honor them. We do this by going in to the space inside—into the heart—and seeking an encounter and chance to wrestle with what that cairn represents. What does this thing say about God, about waking up.

We ask ourselves what this marker offers us in order to be in union—NOW. When we have woken up, we should add a stone to the marker. When we have found Him, we should add a stone to the pile.

Every cairn is an image of the Great Cairn. The Great Cairn is our beloved heart-space. Being awake is the multi-dimensional awareness of all phenomena being present throughout all time in that space. The point that is our heart is the endless space of the Divine Milieu. We have the opportunity to meet God at every moment because meaning is layered on meaning throughout all creation. Everywhere we go we have arrived.

∽ ∽ ∽

UNDER EVERY ROCK

I am looking
under every rock
I find -
for something.
I am not sure
what it is
right yet.
I have been told
that I will
know it when I
find it,
when I see it,
or smell it
I will know.
I cannot help
but wonder
if I have forgotten
 I am searching.
Turning rocks

is just
such fun.
What is it I am doing
again? Am I
looking for rocks,
or somehow looking
for myself?

It is remarkable how each religion finds its own way to image the heart and the journey within. We all build places to mark off encounters and wrestlings with God. Everyone has them.

Monks' cells carved in sandstone and limestone cliffs, stone huts built along glorious pilgrimage vistas, cairns piled high to mark off the sacred, shrines along roads and trails, large stones in a field, they are all markers of the heart. "Something of importance happened here", the cairns call out. "Stop and remember what these rocks stand for", the rocks cry out.

All of these places shadow the interior space we go to when we pray. All of them give us an outward nexus from which to make an inward journey. All of them remind us that we know our ultimate solace comes from meeting the One in the silence of the heart. The outward "holy places" of the religious person are really emblems of the heart. They mark a place on earth where someone found the path in; they show everyone that "It happened here. I found God here." It may be a garden, it may be statue, it may be a cross by the side of the road; whatever it is, it offers us hope.

We all need a place outside of us that images our inner heart. We need to create places that sign for us to go within—NOW. We need spaces that are caves of the heart. We do not need to wait for them. We have them now. They are this moment. They are this place. We need to learn how to feel confident enough to sanctify this moment in time and this place in space.

There is a need to show everyone that holy occurrences happen in space and time. There is a need to show ourselves. We mark them to help us remember that time and space were altered by a meeting and wrestling with God; that we were changed in a meeting and wrestling with God. We mark them to remind us that union is possible. Cairns at holy places scream out, "Someone opened up to God here. You can, too." Our hearts groan with this longing intent. Our lives clamber toward this hope of meeting.

The landscape all around a cairn—all around a heart—is changed by the Presence of meeting and wrestling with God. Moses' face shone with the Glory of the LORD. People were healed in the Presence of Jesus. We are born-again when we engage God.

Sometimes the words we share in this discussion will feel forced or just a bit beyond comprehension. What we are trying to work with here in this text is the notion that all space and time come to bear on this moment and this place. We can unite with God here and now. That takes bringing together both the local and the non-local. Of course this will be tough. We will have to sustain the power of juxtaposed positions and images. Bear with it. Treat it as poetry and let the words roll over you, creating an impression that is itself the meaning.

When we are talking about caves, chapels, cells, prayer rooms, and cairns we are talking about sacred space, "walled off" or "set aside areas." They are markers in space and time. These are sometimes called "hermetic spaces."

Hermes shows up over and over again in these types of discussions because of his birth in a cave and his re-swaddling of himself as an infant (after he stole his brother's cattle). The cave and swaddling are walled-in notions. It is that sense of seclusion (cave-like) and surrounded-ness (swaddled-ness) that keeps Hermes name close to these settings. He is seen as the "god" of the interior and interior quest.

The heart is an Hermetic space. It is the interior place for meeting and wrestling with God. The heart is a walled garden, a cave fed by an underground spring, a hollow in the side of a rock, and the shade of a sheltering pine. Set apart, it is Holy unto the LORD. It is a comfort object from before all time.

Hatefulness tends to produce hatefulness, love tends to produce love, and humility tends to produce humility. How can we transform the places we go to for prayer? How can we transform the inner chapel of our hearts—change them to reflect the Glory of the One? How can we mark the landscape of our lives with the wrestling encounters we have with the Uncircumscribable One from all ages? How may we discern the meaning of the landscape?

My hope is that we will begin to look at the markers of meaning in our lives and notice how we store that meaning in our heart. My hope is that we will begin to see that heart as a multi-dimensional universe within us that is truly already the Divine Milieu. That we will begin to use the meaning all around us to wake up to what IS.

My pragmatic desire is that we will look at places we set aside as holy. We will reconstruct our prayer life and the shape of our interior world. We will recognize the impact things have on us and discriminate toward health. In addition, that ultimately we will WAKE UP to the presence of God in us.

Our journey in this book will be more like an amble or a wandering. We will hop from pillar to post looking for meaning and attempting to infuse things with meaning. We will look at our practices and the practices of those from our shared human past. We will begin to notice that there is a hidden depth to how we live—one that reveals we live in layers or dimensions, not simple and flat lines.

Whether the spaces of prayer are inside or outside they reveal and transform who we are and who we are becoming. Join me as we amble among the markers and choose to transform space and time by hallowing our prayer closet within. The prayer closet of our heart.

Let us find the things that we have left as markers all through our lives and those markers that have been left by others in the life of the Church. Let us learn to read what they have to tell us about where we have been, where we are, and where we are going. Let us become changed into the very image and likeness of the One who has called us from the beginning of time and space. Let us also leave holy markers for all who come after.

CHAPTER ONE

WATERING THE GARDENS AT the beginning and the end of the day has been an activity that has peppered my life from youth. It is relaxing. It also feeds me in ways other activities do not. It has been a cairn in my life since childhood. It has been a sacramental landscape for meeting God. It has taken me into my heart.

When I am about the task of watering gardens, I am reaching back into my life and doing something that is self-soothing and connective. It integrates the disparate pieces of my life. It is wholesome for me.

My life is a train of stories of watering gardens. I can remember watering gardens as far back as elementary school. In all of that practice, I have learned to be in God's Presence as I water. The magnitude of repetition over the years has been a force capable of establishing union with God through this simple act.

Some years I take to watering much more regularly than other years. It has partly to do with the gardens I plant and the needs they have for water-flow. It is also connected to the fact that some years are naturally wetter than others and require less garden tending from me—"the waterer." Sometimes I simply water because I need to: it is good therapy.

However often I water, I am reminded of the tending that needs to accompany all forms of life and growth. I am reminded how I am tended by the "Gardener of Souls." Watering helps me conform to His image and likeness. Watering nourishes my heart-space. Watering is an activity that sacramentally transforms my life—when I am attentive to the process.

One particular season had called me to the task of watering more often than in years past. That year I learned to love the routine for its calming affect in a new way: the sound of water, the greenery, and the repetition of a simple task. It soothed me and gave me peace. I learned a lot from the regularity of the task that year. I learned from mindfully practicing the art of watering.

≈ ≈ ≈

STONE CAIRNS

I have piled stones,
one on top of another,
for decades now.

Fingers
slipping over rough
granite -
my heart
is settled in
simple tasks.

I have piled
stones of habit
over the days
of my journey.

Praying is a stone.
Watering herbs
and gardens of flowers
is another stone.
Hymns and chants
and acts of
kindness are stones,
too.

My words
have become stones
I pile to settle
my heart.

Long ago,
across the pond,
in Scotland
and on the isles of

the Hebrides
they piled stones
to find the same
simple way on earth.
One pile marks
a grave. Another marks
a battle. Still another
marks a place
where prayers poured forth,
where words pierced
God and His
heart and
His universe.

There is a rhythm
to rock on rock,
a sound
that fills the
heart with the comfort
of familiar sound,
familiar passage.

I bake my bread
and brew my soups
because they are stones
of comfort for
this man's heart.
I water my gardens
and read my books
because they help me pile
stone on stone.
Listening,
reflecting,
encountering,
wrestling
each stone
placed down firmly
on another stone.

These piles of stones
have something to
say about who I am
and where I have been.
These stones are my heart.

The thing that most presented itself to me that particular year of watering, was what I learned from the praying mantises. They taught me the art of slowing. They showed me an image of watchfulness and waiting, of discrimination and patience. While watering, I was able to silence enough of my inner chatter to focus on my surroundings as the water flowed, saturated the earth, and beaded on the leaves and flowers. I watched the mantises on the rise. I became intensely aware of reality.

The watering flushed praying mantises up and out of the cover of stalk and stem; onto walls, and branches, and posts. Had I not been paying attention, I would have missed them. I would have never seen what they had to teach.

They climbed up trying to avoid the water I was adding to the garden. As they climbed, they would often spot a bug and settle in for the kill. Patiently they would wait for the "perfect" moment before striking. In their rising, nourishment presented itself. They would stop and dine. They watched and waited—like the Wise Virgins of Jesus' parable. They were watchful and alert.

I had the good pleasure to encounter their watching and waiting. Slowly focusing on the meal, almost hypnotizing it before the strike, they would become careful, and lose their place in time to a slowed attention. It was the "Power of the Slowing" that Gerald May wrote about in "The Wisdom of the Wilderness" (HarperCollins Books, NY, 2006). Their slowing to capture food made me pause, pay attention, and enter into the slowing myself. It taught me about what it takes to discriminate and discern the quality and nature of things in my life. Although all things can move us toward union with God, some things pose potential dangers and threats of entanglement that are just not worth risking. It requires watchfulness and alertness to become nourished—to grow.

Slowing helps us to focus and become aware. Nature has a tendency to help us enter the slowing, if we watch her examples in other sentient beings. Could my praying become the same? Could I still myself enough to become observant and watch what would arise from my heart as I watered it? Could I become still enough to see the many options for nourishment all around me: love, joy, peace, patience, goodness, gentleness, self-control, community, forgiveness?

For many years prior to this experience of the mantises rising, we had hatched mantis pods as a family. We would buy an egg casing from the local garden store and leave it out in the backyard in a covered aquarium. As the weeks wore on, we would almost forget it was there, until one day someone would notice hundreds of mantises on the walls of glass. It was hard to believe that so many mantises could be in one casing. They were a shifting mass of life and limb covering the aquarium walls. We would take off the lid and watch them scurry throughout the yard.

There was another time we had watched the mantises. Glinda and I had just begun dating. We hiked the woods and collected scraps of nature to weave into a wreath. We started with grapevine. We wrapped it into a circle. We tucked dried garlic-mustard fronds into the hoop. We tucked in some mullein leaves and sassafras roots. We also wove in a mantis pod. We had no idea what it was.

One night, when we returned to her room, the walls were covered in moving spots. At first we thought our eyes were deceiving us. We thought we saw shifting movement. As we stepped closer, we were assured that we did. Hundreds of young mantises covered the wall. This was an accidental hatching. The hatchings in the aquarium were not.

I am glad that we took the time to hatch them. They gave me pause in their hatching, and a renewed sense of stillness in watching them rise while watering the gardens. For years, we had more praying mantises in our gardens than anyone around. For years, I had a new way of seeing prayer.

Their presence has been a cycle of routine. I have seen their daily morphs and the slow changes that happen to them over time. I have seen how their colors change as summer lengthens and draws to a close. From green to brown they fade. Their numbers decrease throughout the browning, until they leave the yard altogether. Gone.

I could only notice this in the repetition of a daily routine. The routine of watering the garden daily brought me to the mantises everyday. Routine reveals so much about how life is going; how it is moving ahead and how it is standing still. The things we place into our lives on a routine basis have so much power to affect who we become; particularly when we pay close and steady attention to them—over time.

Stepping toward the hose at watering time almost felt as if I was entering a holy place; a place where I would uncover some immense glory. The air that surrounded me during the watering time was palpable. I could feel myself entering into sacred space as one hand reached for the hose and the other hand for the spigot knob. I was becoming an act that would transform all space and time. I became a holy event for a moment. That is the best I can do to describe it. A stillness reigned in the act itself. A sacrament was born. Words about phenomena, union, and the sacred are meaningless. The NOW became Divine Milieu.

As I am crafting the description of these moments—with my words—I remember other moments that time slowed down and stood still long enough for me to become transformed. The birthing of our sons. The death of my father. The boarding of our plane home from Greece.

They all had this numinous quality that not only made me feel alive, but also aware. Stillness prevailed. It was not as if they made me feel aware of any one thing in particular. It was that they made me feel aware of everything, all at once. I owned space and time in these events. I was at one with everything. Life itself became a sacrament; living became a cairn. I realized that whether we slow down or the events of life slow us down, slowing is vital for deepening.

Every time I approached the hose I could almost begin where I left off the last time I had watered. The routine itself had some part in my discoveries. Doing the routine over and over built up some sort of energy within the act itself—an energy of seeing. Layer after layer of meaning is added to the pieces of our lives that we repeat again and again. After a while, I began to slow down as I simply began to approach the routine task. As I thought about watering, I would shift into stillness. Could this be the same with my prayer life?

This intrusion of awareness on a single moment is often revealed in routine events. It may also come as we enter into the fruition of some long awaited moment. It can be a result of a process or an event. The mantises were able to open in me this sacred space because of the routine and regular nature of my watering encounters with them. The birth of my sons opened me to eternity because of the culmination of long hours of anticipation and hope. Both can spawn awakening.

≈ ≈ ≈

Coming into the Presence of the Holy One is the same. We may enter into the Presence through a routine event like daily prayer and contemplation. We may enter into the Presence through a long awaited event like a sacrament or rite of passage—even a crisis. Philosophically we would say that entering the Presence can be facilitated by either a process or an event.

Either way it is the same. We must make space for the encounter and notice the encounter if we are to unravel the meaning of the encounter. We must provide time for the wrestling. Without space and time for the encounter of and union with the Divine Milieu, there can be no reality of the Divine Milieu in our lives.

Like the daily watering that produced an encounter with the mantises, we first strike out to find a place—a garden to water. Once we have come to that place to do the work of "watering" we must learn patience, repetition, and watchfulness. We must look for the markers that will call us into encounter and wrestling. It is the same with our prayer life. We can build up a routine that will begin to settle us, even when we simply think about enacting the routine.

We can begin a habit of prayer that will open our awareness with a simple routine. Finding a daily time and place to sit and remember God is how we begin the "watering of the garden." Set aside a time and a place and then we are ready to begin. We must build a cairn—a place of remembering (space). We must visit that holy place often—again and again (time).

Some people choose a rocking chair. Others a straight back chair. It may be in front of an icon, or window, or in an out of the way corner. It may be on a porch, or deck, or shed out back. There may be a "Holy Book" and a candle, or a simple stick of incense. The senses must join the prayer in being able to make this time and this space a shelter from life's usual. But, there must be a place. There must be a place where we can go, sit, and enter into an encounter with Divine union. There must be a place for wrestling with our observing awareness.

When we come to the holy place we have chosen we can begin by offering a simple spiritual practice—a simple prayer. This may be an invocation of the Presence, it may be a sacred salutation, it may be a favorite prayer, it may be a prayer service (like Morning Prayer, or Vespers), or it may be a Psalm.

Once the words are offered, it is as if we have drawn a line around our place, we have marked it. "This is sacred space, this is sacred time" our prayer tells us. We have added another stone to the cairn. Eventually we will learn to sit and inhabit the stillness of that time and space itself, but at the outset, we must have a spiritual practice of prayer that we can begin and return to in our sacred place. We must have a "watering act."

It is important to find a space that you can return to with little or no distraction. You are going to return here daily—perhaps even more often. The time you spend here will be like the "watering of a garden." It must be routine and it must be thoughtful.

There are a myriad of practices you can pick up in this space. First, going to this place must become a regular habit—a routine visiting. Second, our spiritual practice in this prayer-space must become a regular habit—a routine visiting.

Go to this place often and just begin with a prayer (or a psalm, or a prayer service) and conclude with a sitting in silence. Remind yourself that you are here to water the soul, to commune with the Divine. Let what comes to fruition in your silence be a natural out-flowing of what your heart, mind, and soul hold inside after offering up your spiritual practice.

Let your sitting begin with a practice. When the practice is finished, simply sit. Become aware of your own presence in this cairn. Become aware of what the stones of practice are building. Listen. Watch and wait for what arises as you water the garden of the soul.

The more we visit this space, the more meaning it will have for us. When we pass by it, we will sense the history it has in our lives and it will begin to have a feel all it's own. It will radiate a sense of identity to us. We must return to this cairn-space over and over again.

Our thinking does the same. When we have a thought over and over again, it builds up a sense of identity in us. We collect whole bunches of associations around the things we think.

Perhaps we have the thought of "apple pie." As we think of "apple pie" over the years, we will begin to attach experiences of "apple pie" to the idea. Perhaps we think of grandma's pie, or our mother's. Perhaps we remember the permeating aroma. We may have intense autumnal memories when we think of "apple pie." Maybe we are galvanized by the texture and flavor of the crust.

We add to the thought of "apple pie" the memories, feelings, impressions, and inner tastes that go along with all of the pies we have experienced. These things get all glommed together. Images and impressions begin to affect our perceptions. In time, depth is added to an idea. We develop multiple layers of meaning. A thing (or the idea of a thing) becomes a concept.

This concept carries much more weight than the simple beginning idea of "apple pie." The concept becomes our icon of "apple-pie-ness." Eventually, all of the surrounding associations that go along with "apple pie"—crust, grandma, autumn, smells—become a part of the history of "apple pie" in our lives. All melds into concept.

Neuro-scientists tell us that this familiarity and development with and of an idea or thing is very real. Repetition of phenomenal contact enhances meaning. The brain selects toward protecting thoughts and experiences that express familiarity because of regular and routine exposure or encounter. Things we experience over and over again get protected in our neural processes.

The axons in the brain transmit neural messages. The dendrites in the brain receive neural messages. The path these thought/messages travel between the two is called a neural pathway. Each time we have a particular thought or sequence of thoughts, the body wraps a myelin sheath around the neural pathway this thought travels (making the connection stronger and more readily accessible).

The subsequent thoughts that emerge from our initial thought also begin to develop neural pathways as well. A system of associative connection is built—a superhighway of meaning and understanding. Firing off certain thoughts may automatically trigger groups of thoughts, entraining them together based on their repetition and proximity.

When we have the thought of "apple pie" a pathway is created from the idea that spawned the notion of "apple pie", to the image we have of "apple pie", and then (perhaps) to our memories of specific apple pies from our past. The firing of the neurons for the thought of "apple pie" become entrained with these other associative images mentioned in our above thought scenario and they begin to learn to fire in sequence together. Perhaps we tend to think of Grandma (who made the best apple pies) when we think of apple pies, or of autumn (since we tend to make apple pies during harvest time).

Soon, all of the associative images we have for an idea get glommed in with the circuitry of meaning that we weave for that thing. We may not be aware of the connections we have made, but "apple pie" sure feels like grandma and autumn to us for a reason.

The myelin sheath that wraps the pathway of transmission is a lipid. It is made of fat. Repetition of thoughts and sequences of thoughts actually strengthen the pathway and the likelihood of relying on this pattern in the future. More myelin sheathing is wrapped around a pathway each time it is traveled. A neural cairn is born. Repetition of neural firing strengthens the likelihood of survival. Thoughts in close association tend to enter into the firing sequence of the neurons.

This is why we tend to associate one thing with another. It is why we sense autumn's approach when we notice a shift in the intensity of the sun's rays. Something inside is connecting these things together.

A symbiotic bond is formed between ideas we have that seem to go together. When one idea fires off down a neural pathway, it may trigger the firing off of other associated ideas. We may have wondered why in the autumn we always long for apple pie. It may be attached to the changing of the leaves in our memories. When autumn arrives and the leaves change, patterns and associations are fired off in our hearts and minds.

So it is with prayer spaces. Slowly over time we add all of the experiences we have had in this place—and others just like it—to the idea of this space. We build up a concept of prayer space. We plant, water, and nourish the notion of prayer. A cairn-space is created.

It does not take long to be able to build up such a deep and expansive notion of prayer space that it becomes portable. We no longer need to enter the exact first space of prayer, we may then simply enter the concept that has been built over time. We surround our prayer with the myelin-like sheath of repetition. We learn how prayer time may become a peaceful encounter.

Once this peaceful encounter is hardwired into us, we may be able to enter into prayer and its subsequent peace-space in a new location. Once we do that, then this new location gets added into the repertoire of prayer-peace. Cairns become linked together. But we cannot hardwire these notions together unless we have a regular and routine practice of these experiences that will ensure the myelin sheathing necessary for cellular familiarity.

It becomes possible to enter into prayer space, then, while in the grocery line. We can go into our sacred place while in church pews, stuck in traffic, or while rocking our tired new-born to sleep. This is only possible if we start with a specific place and go there for specific times—repeatedly. We must build this space in our world and in our interior lives. We must visit it often, to make the impression stronger. We build, one stone at a time. Once this happens we can add new associations, new places to the pathways of prayer that begin to fire when we settle ourselves into prayer.

Over time we will begin to notice what is going on in this space. Like being able to watch the mantises rise from the plants to find a meal and safety, we will observe thoughts and feelings arise in our space. We will sense patterns and themes arising from our heart. We will hear cries of love and desperation climbing out of our interior to the One Who Is. We will recognize patterns and smaller cairns. Over time.

Perhaps when we sit to pray, we get fidgety at first. If we do not find something to do to calm this fidgetiness, then we will be hardwiring fidgetiness into our prayer associations. We will find ourselves getting fidgety whenever we pray. So we find an antidote to the fidgetiness and we apply it.

This is why it is suggested to have something to do in our prayer spaces, something to bring us back around to our center. This ensures that "centeredness" is hardwired into our neural firings and not "fidgetiness."

We start by finding a time and place. We add a habit of prayer. We return to that time and place again and again. We use our habit of prayer—our spiritual practice—to settle us and begin new neural associations. We sit, we practice, we enter the slowing.

So far we have looked at a simple prayer practice to help us do this. If once we have said our prayers and sit in silence we find that we are distracted in a thousand directions, we cut off that experience by returning to the prayers again.

We retrain our distractions by replacing them. We sit, we pray, we slow down into stillness and when the slowing is disturbed by a thousand and one random thoughts, we go back to our prayer and try to approach stillness again. We build better neural pathways.

We can choose to reroute all of our arising thoughts and feelings in prayer. When we do this, we are structurally changing the types of ideas and notions that we allow to fire in the sequencing associations of our interior life. If anger arises we can learn to hear it, trace it to its roots (perhaps jealousy or hatred) and then cut it off with the antidote of returning to our prayer. If discord arises, we can learn to hear it, trace it to its roots (perhaps lust or spite) and then cut it off with the antidote of returning to our prayer.

What we are doing in this work of returning to prayer and a re-approach of the stillness is helping us to learn new ways to process our emotions and thoughts. We are wrapping myelin sheaths around new associations we have built. Once we have done this for a while, we will have learned a process of helping our mind deal with distractions. Eventually it will slow down and tire, allowing us to enter silence in a fuller way.

Slowly, over time, the things of the heart may be transformed. We may replace one habit with another; one response with another. Slowly, repetitiously, over time. Just like building a cairn one rock at a time; habits are developed and built one neural transmission at a time. The more we repeat these processes, the more they are imbedded in our lives because of the protective myelin sheath that wraps them.

The wiring of our neural pathways is plastic enough that we shape it by the choices we make in our thoughts, actions, and words. It becomes more and more hardwired with each repetition of the routine. Every act, and thought, and hope is just as plastic.

A garden is nurtured by watering over time. It comes slowly. It comes gradually. It comes in a deep and regular commitment to the garden. So too, does our habit of prayer. First, we find a space and enrich its presence by shaping it into an area for and of prayer. Then, we shape its character and energy by coming to it often: to sit, to pray—offering some practice, to listen to God, to watch what arises in the stillness of our heart.

This is how we build. Our heart is becoming fashioned in the image of our habit.

Chapter Two

Uncovering growth and nurturance from the routine practices of daily life has long been a reality passed on from generation to generation. It is responsible for the development of "tradition" in faith, philosophy, art, politics, and the sciences. It is how we learn what is passed on. Repetition builds continuity. It is a neural thing. It also helps us open to greater things. Laws are fashioned by it, and organizations are developed because of it. Routine practices keep us moored to the safety of the dock of life.

The notion of routine practice has its bearing on our individual daily lives. We live each day enacting patterns or habits that we have allowed ourselves to accept as meaningful. We go as far as to say that a day has been worthless because we have not checked off one of the habits we hold dear. But, are these habits all necessary? Are they all nourishing? Discernment would tell us, "No."

We get up everyday and have a cigarette with our coffee. The pattern, over years, weaves itself into the meaning of what we call "morning." The need for the nicotine is wrapped around the need to repeat familiar events and we are hooked on a habit that we cannot shake. We watch the news before we go to bed. The pattern, over years, weaves itself into the meaning of what we call "bedtime." The need for tantalizing headlines is wrapped around the need to repeat familiar events and we are hooked on a habit we cannot shake. We know these things are not healthy for us, but we have woven them into our expectations.

We must develop patterns that feed us and strengthen us. We must look for the things we need as divine creatures and build them into habitual routine. This way (just like returning to the prayer practice when distracting thoughts arise) we can return to our core and avert building unhealthy routines. These habits entangle themselves in both our biochemical make-up and our cultural patterns of living. They can be at once a physical driving need and an emotional attachment. Habits and routines can ride the crest between the body and mind continuum.

Prayer is needful. Silence is needful. Compassion is needful. Rest is needful. The practices we develop around these needful things should reflect nourishment, health, and wholeness. If we do not routinely make room for the needful things in life, they will not just happen upon us. We do this by wrapping them in the myelin sheaths of repetition.

The same sort of practices should also be present in our lives together—as the body of Christ. Fashioning sacred space and filling it with the heart and essence of prayer is not a journey for the individual alone, it is a corporate practice as well. Having prayer space and prayer time is good for the one; it is also good for the many.

In a day and age when people would like to lose any connection to a daily routine and be set free to experience one new event after another (at least in our own estimation), the need for a nourishing daily routine is great. Having a heart center and a routine visit to that heart center is vital to an emerging stability and health. It is something we can practice together and apart. It is something we can build into the positive associations of what it means to be the Body of Christ.

Although people may verbally acknowledge that routine is not necessary or a healthy requirement in daily life, they do enact the need for routine on a daily basis. People often enact things they need even if they cannot make a verbal or cognitive assent to the importance of the task.

They may not turn each day to the sacred routines of old—prayer and or liturgy, but they do turn to the routine of reading email, checking social media, and watching the news. We find comfort in routines. Unbeknownst to most, we crave routine and create it whether we know it or not. Routine finds a way in our lives until we are able to recognize and give voice to the need. It is a myelin sheath sort of thing.

Routine is a cairn. Routine is a marker in time and space that helps us to know where we are, remember where we have been, and gain a sense of identity as we visit it again and again over time. Routine digs down deep below the structure of past, present, and future; into the reality of the eternal sense of NOW. Routine is a bridge that unites the dimensions of time and space.

We transmit the signal from axon, to dendrite, through a neural pathway wrapped in fat. We pile the rocks—stone on stone—leaving a visible mark in space and time. Have we discerned the soundness of the stones? Why were they placed? What do they sign?

Liturgy, tradition, and prayer are cairns. They help us gain perspective in landscape of life. They mark how far and how close we come and go as we journey. They are a gauge. And, by their nature they are seen as repeatable events. We do them over and over again, wrapping them in meaning and depth. We can do these things as individuals and as a corporate body.

Today, however, tradition and routine have become suspect in Churches. At the same time the Church today is reeling from the need young believers have to find a tradition and routine to envelop them and hold them fast amid the dizzying changes of modern life.

The youth wonder why there are not more secure markers that can help them find their way to God. They long for mentors to show them the stones they have piled and just what they mean. They want to know which things are moveable and which things must not be moved. They want to see islands of stillness among the dizzying advancements and excitements of the digital age.

Having abolished as many routines as possible in the need to modernize, the Church has lost its connection to the ropes that moor her to the community of Jesus throughout the ages. They have toppled the rock piles that others used to view how far they had come and in which direction they should continue. They have dissolved the myelin sheaths that once gave meaning to the life of the believer.

There is a phenomenon of neural pruning in the brain that occurs several times in our lives. Weak or unused neural pathways are removed via a neural wash. All of the pathways that have not developed a thick enough coating of myelin cannot withstand the wash. They are taken away; dissolved. I fear the Church has removed some of its own vital neural pathways. It has removed some habits and routines that give us meaning.

In a very real sense, the removal of routine from our lives is a dismantling cairns on the landscape. Eventually, when you have removed all the cairns and leveled the landscape completely, you have literally taken away all visible means of navigation—with the exception of the heavens. Let's face it, you can't get anywhere that way. You need markers on earth to triangulate with the stars in the heavens. We must have something from which to gain our bearings.

We are finally recognizing that the sparkling appeal of power-point and sound equipment may not provoke in us the same wisdom that emerges from silence and contemplation. We are beginning to question whether strategic plans and mortgages are necessary for enacting community.

There is a deepening that comes in the absence of glitter. It is a deepening that our leaders have not learned how to teach us, but that we are sensing that we need. We have replaced one form of transmitted signal with another form of transmitted signal. Only the new signal may not be as healthy as the old. Are the neural pathways we accept as "Church" the proper pathways; or would discernment reveal another way.

The variables of sacred routine, or the objects of routine may differ from person to person, denomination to denomination. But, there are some core values under the variables that must be addressed. These values are silence, stillness, integration of the senses (the way a solemn chant or hymn can move us to tears), yearning, community, hope, love, prayer, forgiveness, and resolution. People need the routine of being able to enter into sacred space to encounter God and become transformed; not simply to titillate the senses with novel ideas and the latest trend.

Worship and Church need to be about Sabbath rest and wholeness. Church and worship are all about the seventh day of creation. They are rest from the work of life. We need to find ways to enter into the stillness God has called us into—out of the chaos of our worldly lives. The sacredness of Church and worship sets them apart as "Sabbath experiences." Where is the rest in Church today? We cannot envelop wholeness without it.

Sabbath rest is also about telling tales. We reach into the ken of stories that emerge from our history as a people of God and we share them in a space rich in silence and stillness. The space provided by the silence and stillness enables us to hear how the tales interact with our own lives. We connect in a richer fashion when our tales our told out of rest, rather than constant movement. By removing these standard and routine practices from "Church", "Sabbath", and "religious" experiences, we have begun to dismantle structures in the neural ganglia of mankind. We are pruning out developmental culture and its place in our lives. This is dangerous.

Replicating our workplace environments in our Churches has proved empty. We really do not want to have executive meetings on Sunday, we just have forgotten that we are being called into something different. Making Churches into businesses has failed in the long run and we all feel that. Relegating growth to an "org chart" has left us hollow. Eventually we are left with asking, "What happened to Jesus in all of this? Where has God gone in all of this?" Perhaps we have substituted our prayer practices with the distractions that keep us from stillness.

As easy as it is to do this in our private lives, it is just as easy to do this in our corporate lives. We can eradicate healthy habits quite nicely in democratic cultures. I am afraid Church has become democratic—in ways that it has clearly not ruminated over long enough.

We know that routine is vital for health. Breathing over and over is healthy; the beating of the heart over and over is healthy. Resting daily is healthy. Eating nutritious foods regularly is healthy. These simple routine and regular events bring us around to stable health. But, breathing in toxins, polluting our bloodstream, sleeping fitfully, and eating junk food are not the same as ingesting healthy routines.

There is no difference in what brings us health as the Body of Christ. We need to breathe, to allow our heart centrality in our lives, to rest, and to be nourished. We would do well to ask ourselves if these things can truly be accomplished in the communities we have allowed the Church to develop into.

Is there a chance for us to breathe when we have allowed congregations to become huge and each member must clamber to be noticed? Is there any place for the healing of our heart when we have created hierarchies and rules of polity that supersede our just being vulnerable with each other before God? Can we find rest when we have fundraisers, mortgages, and programs to worry about instead of compassion and forgiveness? Will we find nourishment just because we employ the latest technology?

These values and these questions lie at the root of the routines we establish. Simply recognizing that we need routine to mend is not enough. We must walk away from the process of routine—step back—and ask ourselves what we are called into as a people when God calls us to be restored in Him.

Building this kind of wisdom into our routines of gathering and worship would become signposts and markers we would pass on to our children and theirs after them. If we talked about the "cairns" that remind us of who we are and who we are called to be with any degree of depth, we might actually challenge our communities to strive against the dumbing-down of the holy life.

Where in the life of the Church do we find the oversight that comes from a rigorous spiritual formation and direction? Where is the discernment of the health of our habits? Who is taking the pulse of the congregational practices? Why do we allow "garbage in" and expect "gospel out"? Who will stand up and say, "We need time around a fire to simply sing and tell the ancient tales"? Where are the prophets? And, are we listening to them?

For too long the Church has been held hostage by the "old-guard" members that sit in the back and make rude comments about what people are wearing when they walk to the altar, or demand we only do what we have always done—without questioning the strength and accuracy of the neural pathway? Is this worshipping in spirit and in truth? The nay-sayers have taken charge, demanding that we do things the way we have always done them without questioning whether these things are nourishing. Why have we allowed this habit to build a myelin sheath over the neural pathways of the Bride of Christ? How have we gotten down to this?

I am afraid that before we even developed the technology or the words to go with the technology, that someone has hacked into the Church and stolen our true identity.

When we walk through the woods, it is common to have deep, mystic, and awe-inspiring realizations. We have moments of wonder as we wander through the beauty of creation. Marking the places where God clearly touched us and spoke to us is an ancient craft. Piling one stone on another as a remembrance of experience is old. We join a long line of cairners when we create memory-piles of rocks. These mounds remain to offer us hope that we can be moved, we can be invigorated, and we can be revitalized. It happened in the past—it can happen again, now. That is what cairns call us into.

Jacob piled stones at the place of his meeting with God. He marked the place of his epiphany dream (of angels ascending and descending on the ladder) with an altar of remembrance. The entrance to the garden of Eden was marked off with Cherubim. The Holy of Holies was marked off with a veil. In each case, something is made present to slow us down and ask us to remember what we are doing here.

How have we allowed this into our gatherings today? What markers slow us down? How have we learned to recognize the rising of the mantises?

It used to be that sacraments were this type of signpost. The words and acts of sacramental rites were meant to slow us down. We were meant to review our lives and who we had become. Awe and reverence punctuated our gatherings. We were asked to allow God's Person to meet us and change us. Do we still find the same meaning and purpose in our rites today? Have we instead, "traded up" for more special effects and glitz; less depth?

What cairns are we establishing as a modern Church? How will the children we raise remember the encounters and wrestlings we allowed? Will we be marked off as the cairn of structural ineptitude? Will we be memorialized as the virgins who fell asleep in the Light of God's Presence—unprepared and out of oil? Will we pass on the tradition of being held captive by thoughtless and unholy banter?

Cairns are meant to make us stop, to look, to remember encounters and wrestling, and to ultimately enter a Sabbath rest. Can we build new cairns for the people of Jesus that come after us? The old ones—all too often—do not offer life.

"CREEDS"

I used to know the
creeds and words
to songs that gave
me ways to know
who God was and
was not.
Stones were all
around on
the landscape
of the Church
showing me turns
and pointing me
toward directions
I believed I should
travail—places
I was told were safe.
Now, I stand here

staring at
all of the horizons
around me
hoping,
beyond all hope,
someone has not
taken down all
the signs
I knew
when I
was younger.
"Light of Light"
is gone.
"True God
of True God"
is gone.
Hardly anyone
says the word
"begotten" anymore.
No one says,
"Begotten not made" –
no,
not one.
I almost have forgotten
how to pronounce
"Athanasios,
Hippolytus, and
Hesychios."
I very rarely hear
their names
at all
anymore.
How can we have
erased the foundation
upon which every
generation before us
has stood?
How can we have toppled

the pillars that
support the roof
over our spiritual
heads?
Do we really feel
that we alone
have made the
only offering to God
that He accepts?
Or have we,
like Cain,
killed our brothers -
because of their success?

I climbed the hill; the hill to the upper woods. I went to the cairn I built for Saint Columba. I call it Colum-Cille. "The dove of the Church."

The rock pile sits on a huge rock on a small knob that rests on the side of a hill at the top of the mountain. It is a stone pile that gives me peace. Like the prayer rocks of Appalachia, Colum-Cille is a place I come to pray.

Not far from this rock, thirty-five years ago, I gave my life to Christ. This cairn is charged with meaning for me. All sorts of neural pathways fire in sequence when I am here.

At first, I offer words: praises, litanies, thanksgiving, adorations, and requests. I sing sometimes. Singing our prayers is like praying twice (Saint Augustine). We pray once with our mouth—that is the words of cognition that escape from the mind. We pray once with our song—that is the melodies of emotion that escape from the heart.

After the words have escaped, after the melodies have left me, I sit. I sit in silence. I sit in a silence filled with nothing. There is often a listening that occurs. Most often, there is a simple being with God that transcends all form. I sit in that rest and I AM. I have a being, and it is rooted in God.

When I leave this place, I am always changed. The mounting meaning from days gone by crashes into the place I stand today.

Two days later, I climbed the hill again. This time I had my oldest son. It was the day of his confirmation. In the Church we honored his commitment to Jesus with a litany and a vow to see him through. We did this for all of the youth who made their love of Jesus known to us.

On the hill, I was honoring Jesus' commitment to him. I thanked God for doing a great work in Zachary. I laid my hand on his head and prayed for his infilling. I taught him what cairns are and how to build them. I took him in to cairn-space. He knows the meaning this hill holds for me. It holds that now for him.

When we left that place, we were changed.

In the field of Project Management, projects are managed by applying the nine management areas over the entire life of a project. The nine management areas fit into a standard process so that you can be sure to arrive at your destination on time and within budget. There are antidotes for errors that may arise all along the way.

One of the nine management areas is Scope Management. Managing scope is making sure that everything you are doing is really related to the project and its completion and not some mutant topic that has emerged along the way to derail the project and all of its resources.

Any one who has managed a business project knows how easy scope can be skewed if it is not constantly monitored. This shift in the focus of scope is called "creep."

The question that scope managers ask is, "does this project include all the work required to complete it and only the work required?" It is an important question to be asked when drawing up a project plan and when analyzing the ongoing progress made in the project.

Scope Management is really what we are talking about when we refer to eliminating things that arise in life that are not related to our spiritual practice and stillness. When alternative thoughts arise in our spiritual practice or stillness, we ask if they fall within the purview of our scope. Do these things help us achieve our goals, or do they cause "creep" away from our desired outcome?

Hundreds of thousands of things enter our life that could easily draw us away from our desire to have a spiritual practice and times of stillness. Scope helps us to guard our heart and be watchful. Scope is vital for the corporate as well as the private spiritual life. How do we monitor the scope of the Church today? How much "creep" has crept in and carried away the scope?

When greed arises, we trace it to its roots and then remove it; turning again to our spiritual practice so we can enter the stillness. Does greed belong in our stillness? If it is beyond the scope of our time of prayer, it is removed. This habit of pruning is necessary for our individual spiritual life and practice as well as for our corporate spiritual life and practice.

The watchfulness and "guarding of the heart" that we learn to help us prune our personal growth is the same watchfulness and "guarding of the heart" that we need for the Body of Christ. It must remove thoughts, patterns, habits, and associations that do not fit within the scope of our mission.

This cannot be accomplished by one person in the Body of Christ. It requires a group that is willing to wrestle with the notions that exist in the Church today; notions that may be good, but not in keeping with what is required. The larger we allow "Church" to become the more we increase the chances that "creep" can enter our processes.

We acknowledge the idea of discernment in our personal growth by developing processes that help us decide what is good and wholesome for us to do. We cut out things (hopefully) that interfere with our personal development. How will we figure this same process into the life of the Church? How will we enact corporate watchfulness and "guarding of the heart"?

Pruning neural pathways is essential, but as we can see from our history, you can cut out the wrong things. Will we acknowledge and enact a process of selection in time to keep the Church from totally walking away from conscious development? Or will we prune ourselves into a theological wasteland; dumbing-down our faith until it is useless?

Can we make cairn-space something we teach our youth? Can we take them into places and times where we reach out to God and meet Him and wrestle with Him? Can we show them how stone is piled on stone? Can we offer to them whole ganglia of neural pathways—routines and practice of the inner life that are so well myelinated that they can grow beyond our own advancements and include their own neural faith development into the circuitry we have passed on through time? Where is the Holy Spirit in this?

Chapter Three

"CAIRN-LOVE"

I have learned
to love the way
rocks are
piled on rocks.
Ambling skyward,
marking the place
in time
when I felt the
freshness of
a snowdrop
open me to the
Holy One.
Holding
my memory in place
to the day
I was broken open
and cried in repentance,
remembering my sin,
being forgiven
for the first time
all over again.
That pile
of rocks
holds eternity
inside.
It is my
place of
departure each

time I pass.
It is my desert,
my place
of indwelling.
I climb
from its simple
peak to heaven
by entering
into the
room
within –
the room
that holds the
memory of
my explosive joy
at my sons' births;
the chamber
that harbors
the pain of
my suffocating horror
when my
father ended his life,
the dwelling place
that shelters
the warmth in
my heart
seeing the
sparkle in
my Glinda's eyes.
There is so
much there
in that pile of rocks.
If I stand with them,
if I sit with them
for a while
and listen to
who I am and
where I have been.

If I touch
the encounters
and wrestlings
I have known
throughout
my time
on the
landscape of
this life lived
I can hear
His whispers.
Sometimes He
asks me to remove a stone,
to get rid of it
or move it to a
different cairn
where it is more useful.
If I sit with
them a while
I move past the
images my mind
recalls and fade
into a clarity
that can only be called
a oneness. I disappear
and the One is left;
my ashes are at the
feet of the One.
I have learned
to love the way
rocks are
piled on rocks.

≈ ≈ ≈

Throughout time, men and women have left the world and built cities in the deserts and in remote places. They have built cairns in time and space devoted to finding God and establishing communities of like-minded folk. They developed landscapes where they could practice their spiritual practice and sit in the silent Presence of the Holy.

Sometimes they built them, only to abandon them because they had gone awry. They discovered they had been built incorrectly. When this happened they moved. They pushed out further into the barrenness of the wilderness. They carried their neural pathways into the furthest extremes of the Empire. They hardwired ways for the faithful to turn within and find the ONE.

The early Christian ascetic movement brought life to the desert. In the barrenness of sand and scrub new life flourished. A paradise was established. What had been empty aridity became teaming with vibrant life. The commitment of the desert ascetics to setting aside a place to meet and commune with God brought life to what was seen as certain death.

The call to finding cairn-space in our lives is the same. Making a place and taking the time to enter into the Presence of God is the transformative action that begins the process of purification, enlightenment, and union with God. We create a sacred-space. We go there often. We perform our spiritual practice. We sit in silent stillness.

We are making the desert flourish with life. We are blazing neural pathways into uncharted territory. We are boldly taking ganglia where no synapse has gone before.

Going into these spaces we create is going into our heart. The heart is the time and the space where purification, enlightenment, and union occur. This same purification, enlightenment, and union are what the desert seekers were searching for. They left the Empire and the newly founded State religion of Christianity because in the absence of "the persecutions" they felt Christianity had become lax. People had pruned the wrong things from the Church.

It was not enough that a few people—the desert saints—escaped the world and set out on a singular journey. Others followed them. They saints had to develop rhythms and routines that would nourish all of the desert dwellers who came to see what was going on out there. They sought to make their communities consistent with the journey to God. This appealed to many.

Abba Anthony (AD 251) heard the words of the Gospel and responded to what he heard. He gave up all he had and moved to the desert because Jesus had said to "sell all you have and give the money to the poor." He set off to live the ascetic call in the desert. He became the "Father of Desert Monasticism" in the Christian tradition.

Abba Amoun (AD 290) married and lived with his wife as an ascetic for eighteen years. His wife finally convinced him to formalize the ascetic calling they had lived by moving to the desert and building up "community." He headed to the desert and founded the ascetic communities at Nitria and Kellia.

Abba Pachomios (AD 292) converted to the faith because of the love the Christians had for one another. He headed into the desert and heard the call of the LORD to stay in one place and struggle. The LORD told him that many would come to him to find their way. He founded the first community at Tabbenesi, and became a spiritual father to many.

Abba Macarios (AD 300) left the world and founded the desert community of Scetis. He learned most of his asceticism from Abba Anthony the Great. His writings, homilies, and sayings had a profound impact on the monastic call and those who came to Scetis.

Abba Arsenios (AD 354) asked God how he could best find spiritual well-being. In a first answer to his prayer, he heard the LORD respond "flee men and you shall be saved." Later, upon asking for clarification of God's will, he heard the LORD say, "Hide from men, and live in silence."

With these words and "calls of the heart" the Christian desert movement was planted, watered, and tended. The desert became a refuge for those seeking purification, enlightenment, and union with God. Men and women went to the desert and created sacred space and sacred time within which to meet God and be transformed.

They went to the desert to cultivate the spiritual practices and stillness we spoke of earlier. Their every act was an entrance into cairn-space. They moved in the desert to bring time and space into same reality as practice and stillness. They sought to enter union with God. To be "alone with the ALONE" and "one with the ONE." In this way, the desert bore fruit.

The desert is an icon of the human heart. It is a place outside. It is also a place within. Our temptations and longings are louder in the desert. Going into the desert is going into the heart. Going into the heart is entering the eye of the spiritual storm. Things become clearer there, but almost too clear to bear.

The desert communities were built one monk, one nun at a time. One stone was placed on another, giving God both the time and space "to shelter" into the lives of His beloved. Called to get away and seek stillness, simple men and women became the tabernacle of the Most High God. They learned how to live this heavenly glory and paradise with others who dwelt with them. They shared the singular journey among the many.

The desert saints were trying to retrain the Christian mind to find the core values of Gospel living and Apostolic calling. They were trying to rewire the Church's neural pathways. They were wrapping myelin sheaths around the practice of union with the Divine.

We are called to build the same encounters with the Divine in our own lives. Our heart must flourish like the desert. We must project those encounters back into our communities and the ways we live on this earth place.

We find a place, we go there often. We flee, we hide, we seek silence.

The things we do in our sacred place are themselves cairns. The times we spend and the space itself are cairns as well. All that goes on in this time and this space becomes markers along our neural pathway of Divine union.

Our choices among spiritual practices are many. We may read scripture. We may sing hymns. We may offer prayers or prayer-services. We may do creative visualizations. We may practice lectio divina. We may pray the Jesus prayer. We may fast. We may bow. We may do nothing. There are a thousand and one practices that we can use in our prayer-spaces. All of them take us toward the presence of God.

All of these things we "do" are just the prelude. All of the things we do can help us to approach God (or become purified as the desert fathers would say). They lead us to the place where we can become open to just "being" in God's Presence. We perform the spiritual practice of "doing" first, so we may sit in the stillness of our "being" second.

The "doings" in our prayer-spaces are critical to helping us shed the "world" and all that means. They help us leave behind our bills. They enable us to separate from our cares and woes. They offer us a bridge away from everything that poses as important in our material life. The practices become part of the neural wiring that will lead to our encounter with God.

The practices all give us a place to go back to and start over from when distracting thoughts invade the stillness and silence of consuming the Divine. They are neural ganglia that add layers of meaning to our spiritual development. They lead us to the inner desert; the place of the ascetics where we can flee, hide, and observe silence. They lead us to the place of sold possessions and voluntary poverty of spirit.

But the spiritual practice is just the beginning of what we experience in cairn-space. We also spend time with silence and stillness there. In many ways it is easy to get stuck on the practices we perform in our prayer-spaces. This is not where the deep transformation occurs.

The deep transformation takes place when we lay aside all earthly cares, all spiritual practices, and enter the timeless, and spaceless place of God's presence in our heart. It is here, doing nothing, we are changed by the Spirit.

The space of silence and stillness were very real parts of life in the desert communities. They were nourishing then and there, they are nourishing here and now, as well.

The spiritual practices we use in our "doing" of prayer, really address the redemption of the human nature in us. The Fathers never forgot the great debates over the two natures in man. There is the human nature and the divine nature. We feed the human nature with practices that will help it to approach the Divine One and become aligned with the Holy One.

Purification is the process for our human nature. When we flee and hide, we are entering the process of purification. The practices we use help us return to our beginning when we get knocked off the trail. They rid us of old habits and help us start out again into the barren stillness of the silence of God.

Once we lay aside these practices, we are entering into the "being" of prayer. In this place there can be no action except "actionless action." This is the place of absorbing the Energies of God; a place to simply "be" with the Divine One. Enlightenment and union are the processes for our divine nature. When we seek to enter the silence, we are entering the processes of enlightenment and union.

The desert Christians fasted, prayed, did vigils, and healed the infirmed, but silence and stillness ruled their lives. Without the chance to sit and listen, there could be no activity in their lives. Without plugging in to God's wordless Energies, there was no health. Without stillness, there was no terrain for the unifying encounter.

The human nature needs the spiritual practices to get rid of everything that stands between us and "knowing God." The practices all help us to attain this knowing. These methods all help us to obtain purification.

The divine nature needs stillness to gain enlightenment and union. We do absolutely nothing but hide in the silence. There is no practice or method here; it is an unknowing. This stillness (hesychia) allows God to enter us fully; and us to enter God fully.

We find a place, we go there often. We flee, we hide, we seek silence. When the silence is disturbed, we return to our practice and try to enter the stillness once again. The full spiritual life is a balance between our spiritual practices and stillness.

The monks of the Eastern Christian Church have sought "hesychia"—silence and stillness—with a "passionless passion." Entering into quiet, unobtrusive lives, they have faded from the normal patterns of people on this earth. They hide away in nooks and crannies of the globe, seeking to be alone with the Alone.

The ones who truly arrive at this "desireless desire" are so far askew from the image of holiness we expect to see, that we have labeled them fools. Their sayings and their actions make little sense to we who are so entranced by material reality. We assume it is they who must be wrong.

We fail to see how insane our world truly looks. Just pick up any of the copies of the "Sayings of the Desert Fathers" (the Apophthegmata Patrum) and read a few of the sayings to gain some bearing on the view from the desert. These are the view from prayer-space.

Some pieces of the holy journey into the heart will never make sense to other people. Setting aside space and time to pray to the Invisible One or sit in His presence is beyond the comprehension of many humans. Yet, the Fathers taught that we are only truly human when we enter into this communion with God; without it we are less than the beasts.

To the writer Pseudo-Macarios the true human anthropology is two-fold. There is the exterior man, which is our old man or the old self. Then, there is the interior man, which is our new man or the new self.

In Christ we are transformed and made new. We are made into interior beings. This elevates us above the beasts, above the old self; a little lower than the angels. We develop this interior being, this new self, by meeting God within. We have a human nature and a divine nature.

The Hesychastic Fathers of the Eastern Orthodox tradition spoke of this same dichotomy (human nature—divine nature, old man—new man) in terms of the mind and the heart. We are called (mostly in the Philokalia—the 5 volume text from the Eastern Church on interior struggle and prayer) to place the mind in the heart during prayer. That is, take all of the spiritual practices we employee to gain access and purification before the presence of God, and place them in the stillness of the heart where we shall be granted enlightenment and union.

Go from darkness to light. Go from dancing to stillness. Go from outside to inside. Go from old man to new man.

We find a place, we go there often. We flee, we hide, we seek silence.

There is an peninsula in Greece known as Mount Athos. The "Holy Mountain" or "Garden of the Virgin"—as it is also known—is peppered with monastic houses, kelli (small groupings of individual monastic "cells"), and caves for hermits. Each gathering of monastics has its own "rule of life"; its own way of living together.

Some monks gather often for meals and prayer. Others only weekly. Still others only for major feasts or sporadically. Some monks live their rule alone; completely by themselves.

However they are organized as communities the goal is the same. The monks seek to perform some sort of spiritual practice and also to enter "hesychia"—the stillness/silence of God. There are as many forms for this as there are monks. They truly live in cairn-space.

In the Western Church, Saint Benedict and other "Rule" writers, focused more directly on the pattern of living that monks shared with one another in their monastic enclosures. The "Rules" looked at the apostolic notions hidden in a common life together: how much should people eat, how many items of clothing should they have, how often should they pray, how should they treat guests. Although these "rules" inhabit the communities on the Holy Mountain, they are not the focus of Eastern monasticism. The focus of the Eastern Orthodox monk is tending the heart and making it a place for the Divine meeting. Spiritual practice and stillness: prayer and hesychia. The writing of "Rules" and the living of rules does not predominate.

The work that the monastics perform in their spiritual struggle is seen as therapy. It is what restores them to full health in their lives in the Spirit of God. In Classical times, spirituality and religion were seen as daughters of medicine. The spiritual life was a journey in the healing of the soul. It was a medical science. Today we have all but lost that diagnostic approach to faith.

As you begin to unpack the writings found in the Philokalia—the monastic guidebook second only to the Holy Scriptures—you do get a sense that the writers were addressing illnesses within man. Their spiritual athletics in the arena of asceticism were directed at helping believers to find the antidote and cure for their spiritual illnesses. All of the writings approach spirituality with an eye toward removing the things that block us from becoming whole and healthy in the Spirit.

The writings speak a lot about getting back to a simple practice when we have lost sight of the silent stillness of God. Return to a simple method when you are distracted and start again. Fall and get up. Fall and get up. Fall and get up, again.

This was what they taught as a model for growth. This perpetual return to purification in the life of the ascetic moved them into a place where enlightenment and union could unfold without interruption.

Where much of the Church today has been at a lack for an organized schema or anthropology of man—one that permeates the denominational traditions—the Orthodox Monastic Tradition has maintained a consistent and growing body of knowledge of what it means to be human and how to bring human beings back into rightful homeostasis; centered in God. The path toward wholeness clearly requires spiritual practices and the stillness/silence of God—"hesychia."

The Holy Mountain continues to be a place in space and time in which men still hear the cry of God, "Flee, hide from men, be silent." The monastics believe it is this medicine that will heal the world.

This peninsula is cairn-space. These monks are cairn-space.

Chapter Four

THERE IS A TRADITION of stories told about King Solomon that speak of his spiritual practice of prayer. The stories tell that Solomon carved out a prayer-space around himself with his words, his feelings, and his desires. The stories come from the Sufi tradition. Rumi (Jelaluddin Rumi, AD 1207) is the teller of many of these tales. These tales are about King Solomon's cairn-space.

It is said that Solomon cleared a space around himself and filled it with the escaping power of his intention and love. He cleared a space to make a palace of prayer: words and sighs offered up to the Father.

He found a way to convert time and space into an encountering and wrestling with God. He connected with the Source of All from within his own personal projections. He fashioned the air into a tabernacle of meeting.

It is hard for we modern-folk to recognize that things exist in the "invisibility" of space between objects. Fields exist in these places. Energy exists in these places. Despite our being surrounded by thousands of science fiction stories containing force-fields and energy waves, we are slow to realize that there is something between the electrons of an atom. There is something in the nothingness of space.

There is something present in the nothingness we behold. There is something between particles of matter. There is something between the earth and the moon. We may not see it, but there is something there. Perhaps the "something" that is there has myelin sheaths wrapped around it so information can be passed from one point to another. Perhaps the invisible holds millions of axons and dendrites passing neural data back and forth. Perhaps this whole universe is hardwired with the neural pathways of God; energy moving across the surface of the deep, in matter and in space.

This same field, this same energy surrounds us and permeates us as individuals. It is easy to perceive it on a day when someone is riled up and angry. The air around them is palpable. You can feel the anger. It is the same with mirth. When someone is exuberant with joy, you can feel the joy. We radiate feeling out into the "space" of our own lives; out into our immediate environment. The tenor of the space around us reflects the tenor of the heart.

The Fathers called these fields and energies that surround us and permeate us "logosmoi" (pronounced lo yose mee). Logosmoi are thought-forms. They are our thoughts, emotions, and desires taking shape and form as they dwell within us and as they leave us and enter into the world around us. They are very real.

Perhaps these logosmoi are the angels and demons the desert solitaires wrote about and did battle with in the deserts of Nitria, Scetis, and Kellia. Perhaps these logosmoi are the forces that we battle with in Church when someone leans over and says, "She hasn't been to church since her husband had that affair." Perhaps the logosmoi are what distract us from silent stillness in our prayer-spaces.

We weave a shelter around us with the fields of thought, emotion, and desire we generate from within and project out onto the world. These fields we are weaving create the "me" of our lives. They become what we consider to be the personality. In a real sense they precede us and are still around when we leave. If we fail to cut down an inappropriate logosmoi by returning to our practice, it enters the neural field of our communications about prayer.

Think of the affect certain people have when they walk into a room: some liven things up, while others shut down conversation. Some people exude an atmosphere of love and union, while others exude an atmosphere of distraction and chaos.

Scientists have discovered a whole "mirror" system within us. The mirroring begins with the "mirror neuron" which assumes the behavior and emotion in the immediate environment and then reflects it. Individuals mirror "the other" as if it were themselves. It is how we pick up feelings of conflict and dis-continuity. If someone is saying something with their mouth that they are in conflict with in their heart, their body language will relay that information to us and our mirror neurons will pick up the disconnect. It is that feeling that something does not ring true or is just a bit off.

If we are presenting ill-health and darkened logosmoi, we are setting the tone for the people around us. We are leading them into the valley of the shadow of distraction and separation.

It is believed that the use of language is somehow related to this notion of mirror neurons. Language carries mirroring information and that language is a part of the mirroring process. Emotions are clearly perceived in the mirroring process. Someone walks into the room who is depressed and you can feel the gloom affecting you.

We are not talking about magic. We are talking about the freedom of personal choice. We chose what we will project, but we can also just simply reflect what is all around us. We have control over the things we create in us and project out into the world around us, or we can relinquish control and mirror the world. People can affect the tenor of their own lives. There is a giving and taking in our lives and mirroring neurons are a part of the equation.

Perhaps the greatest wrong we commit on a daily basis is not recognizing that we have the freedom to create—today—the things we choose. We are bound only by what we choose to bind us. We can also choose what we mirror. This day, this moment we do not have to mirror every other day or moment, or even the people around us. We can slow down enough to retrain our neural communications and develop sound and healthy habits and routines.

The process of purification at the outset of monastic therapy (purification, enlightenment, and union) is about purifying the inner man (the human nature) by destroying negative logosmoi and creating positive logosmoi. Spiritual practices help us to remove negative strands from the weaving of our personality and replace them with positive strands. Prayer, fasting, vigils, charity, scriptures, hymns, creeds, prostrations are all tools that work on the purification of the heart of man.

Rumi let us know that daily, Solomon would build a space at dawn made of mystical conversation, intention, and tender compassion: a place within which he could work with his own logosmoi. Rumi called it "The Far Mosque." Solomon created a holy place around him where he could weave heaven and earth together into the fabric of his own personality. He built a prayer-space within which he could meet God through his spiritual practice and then enter into the stillness of the presence of the Most High. He kept within the scope of this ideal by always returning to praise, adoration, wonder, and awe before the Creative Father. He built in positive logosmoi; positive routines.

Solomon is one of the holy ones (in what will become a long tradition from Merkabah mysticism through the Hassidic movement) that

sought to conjoin heaven and earth within himself. The "Far Mosque"—
this prayer-space that King Solomon created daily -was Solomon's place
to flee to; his place to hide and be still.

It is said that all of his wisdom was given to him in this "Far
Mosque." His constructive prayer gave him a place within which to give
and receive. He gave to the All-Wise his adoration and praise. He received back the wisdom of the ages. Because he made a place to give, he
was given to, in return.

Among the wealth of wisdom he received, Rumi teaches that
Solomon was taught the mystic use of all of the plants of the earth during
this time. He was shown which plants healed which diseases. Solomon
emptied himself to God in this space and God filled him back up. He
mirrored the wisdom of the Wise Father.

"A CRYSTALLINE NET AND PALACE OF LOVE"

There was a palace,
one that Solomon built
out amid the myrtle brush
and the line of desert sand.
With each new sun
he would build this place,
greeting
the heavy morning mist
and the new dawn air.
Hands to the sky,
elbows bent,
he called to the Father
of earth, and of air;
he cried to the Father
of the fading moon.
Reaching within,
he grabbed his intentions,
he grabbed his desires
and wove them together,
wove them as one.
He wove them together
with wonder and awe;
wove them together

with words and with humming.
Wove them together
with his davening motion.
Wove them together
with adoration and praise.
Calling heaven
down to the earth;
Calling the Creator
down to creation.
Warping and wefting
them all into one;
a fabric and cloth
that flowed out from
him into the world all around –
a fabric of yearning
for wisdom divine.
"How is it, Holy One,
That the waters return
each moment anew
each morning again–
with power and joy,
dew tenderly glistening
in the morning light?"
"How is it, Master,
that the sun rises again
each day anew
with courage and strength?"
"How is it that You –
Blessed ONE forever–
have given for me to
rebuild this palace of worship,
this edifice of prayer?"
"Where do you
hide the courses of water?
Where have you stored the
hale and the wind?"
His breathing and feeling
would fashion the walls;

his soul and his words
would join them as one.
Shimmering letters
sprang forth into shape;
robust emotion
chambered the air.
His stand in the sand
reflected his heart:
awestruck, humble,
thankful.
All from his
mouth with moisture
and mercy,
words became form
and housed simple
awe. Words built a
chapel for his
meeting with God.
Strengthening, towering
elementals of thought,
mated with powerful
passions, and hopes.
Beckoning,
drawing,
calling
the
shards of the Father
out of the chaos
into one place.
Together conjoining
seen and unseen.
Davening, davening,
shokeling, shokeling
pumping desire
up to the heart
and down from the head.
Niggunim, niggunim
he sings as he bobs,

sprouting songs,
sprouting tunes
from a humming throat,
an expansive heart
that he has
wed
to the core of his being.
"Father, Father,
O Father of mine,
Mold me and meld me,
join with my heart.
He hums and
sings his nonsense
to God –
it reverberates
into all creation.
"Ah, la, la
Ah, ba, ba.
Ah, la, la
Ah, ba, ba."
Simple words,
simple sounds
expressing his love.
"Iffe-deadle-deadle,
iffe-deadle-doo.
Iffe-beadle-beadle,
Affe-beadle-be."
"Sisters of earth,
sisters of air,
join me as witness
to the presence Divine.
"House now
the Holy with
me in one space,
witness the
merger of
heaven and earth."

~ ~ ~

The sacred space of Solomon's "Far Mosque" is the sitting place we create in our own lives. The place we set aside for prayer; the place where we do spiritual battle. We take the time and make a place into which we can go routinely to encounter God and wrestle with Him and with our own selves. We make a palace for prayer and we use our intention, our desires, and our longings to fill the palace. We perform some sort of practice to help purify the old man. We practice and then we move into stillness.

Keep in mind, that what makes the Christian tradition different from other traditions is that we believe our salvation is established, and built by Christ Himself. None of the things we do will earn us that or affect that. The efforts toward purification, enlightenment, and union that we make are all responses that we have to the amazing love of God in Christ. All of this work we are talking about is not to achieve salvation. It is our response to salvation.

Bonhoeffer told us, the only person who could claim salvation as a free gift of God through Christ, is the person who has given up everything to follow Christ. This conundrum is always afoot when we speak of the salvation and the Divine. Salvation is free, but it costs us everything. The spiritual battle is our response to all that God has done for us.

When we look at the kinds of things that Solomon offered up in his holy space, we are reminded that we do not simply come to our cairn-space to give God an agenda of what we want next—our forthcoming acquisitions. The walls of our spiritual space should not be a shopping list for the Divine. We come to encounter, engage, and to wrestle. To get into the hard work of offering ourselves a living sacrifice. We come to praise and adore.

This may mean asking questions about awesome things that have been since the beginning of time. "Where do you house the rain?" "How old are the crevices in the mountain—and just why are they there?" These things seem foreign to us, but are so vital. They are forms of worship. We are acknowledging our empty frailness and utter inability to comprehend the magnanimous depth of the ways of the Creator—"I and Thou." They are signs that we are encountering and wrestling—trying to meet and come to terms with a God that is at once knowable and unknowable. We should struggle to open our hearts and allow humble groanings to escape, as well as offer prayers for forgiveness, adoration, and wonder.

Whatever the routine we enact in this place, we must remember that it sets the tone for who it is we are becoming.

The routine of "humble-heart-groaning"—or any other form of prayer we allow in our prayer-space—is a myelin sheath we would do well to weave into our lives. The more often we repeat a practice in our prayer-space, the more hardwired it becomes in our lives. We will naturally emulate what we have hardwired into our lives. Wondering and being awe-struck in our prayer places is healthy. It is a noble pile of rocks.

Solomon was creating a cell for himself in his morning ritual. Solomon was building for himself an invisible chapel. Solomon was etching a space in time. He was building in the air the same thing that monks and nuns were building in the deserts of Nitria, Sketis, and Kellia. He was building an ethereal cell.

Like Solomon, we go to our cairn-space to perform some practice that will take us into "The Presence." Then, we sit in that presence—silent and still. Whatever we receive from the presence of God is a gift.

"Davening" is praying for the Jew. "Shokeling" is the rocking motion that goes on during Jewish prayer. Back and forth, back and forth the rocking goes. Almost making and invisible space for the prayer to inhabit by pushing the air away from the center. It is more than just a bow to the Divine, it is a way of concentrating and building up to an almost fevered pitch. Many faiths use full prostrations (bowing and then lying prostrate on the ground) as a means of offering homage and creating sacred space.

This sort of physical practice while praying tends to enhance the work of the prayer. It helps to connect the heart and the mind to the words. This is always the struggle we have in liturgical praying: trying to get the heart and the mind on the same page. We use the prayers as a bridge for synchronizing the heart and the mind.

Other things can bring the two together. Shokeling is an attempt to conjoin the heart and mind. Shokeling is the neural pathway between the two. It attempts to bring the two together.

"Niggunim" are the melodies and tunes that are sung or hummed in prayer. A famous "nigun" (singular) is the "yeadle, deadle, deadle, deadle, deadle, dum" of Tevya in "If I were a Rich Man" from Fiddler on the Roof. On some occasions, sensible words accompany the tunes; in others, it is just heartfelt abandon. We make up a sound to accompany the longing. We inject our hunger and yearning for merger with the Divine into little tunes and groans.

Again, the focus is on bringing a sense of emotion to an act. It is bringing the heart and the mind together to be in the presence of the One. It is preparation for stillness. It is a form of alignment, and as such, is an act of purification.

Davening, shokeling, and niggunim are things done as an individual, but by virtue of the fact that they are often performed in groups of people, mirror neurons will enable these actions to affect the community. It begs the question of "Who is responsible for who's actions?" In fact, it reminds people living in community that the choices and actions of their own life do affect other people by affecting the space they all inhabit.

It is not enough to simply set up a practice and enter the stillness. We do need to be concerned about how that affects and alters the community around us and the space that community inhabits. How a cairn is built is critical. The materials used are equally as critical. There is an ethical element to the individual interior experiment. What we do affects those around us. Things are done not for the self alone, but for the life of the "world."

Solomon is a reminder that what we do does matter. We gain wisdom when we enter into the humility of one who offers awe and wonder. Could the absence of awe and wonder be at the root of why we have established so many darkened logosmoi in community settings? Has our failure to adore kept us from receiving the wisdom of the Loving Father? When we have focused on lesser things, have we received lesser things in return?

Perhaps Church has become a mirroring of prunable pathways.

CHAPTER FIVE

SILENCE CAN BE UNNERVING. Stillness can be unsettling. We all know how difficult it is to sit quietly without moving. There is no wonder why it has been written out of most church services and spiritual gatherings.

Because it is difficult; however, it does not mean it should be abandoned altogether. Perhaps we need to learn to become familiar and even comfortable with silence and stillness. Perhaps we can slowly build up neural associations with this dimension of the Divine Milieu.

Simply saying to the Father of Lights, "This is really uncomfortable. I have not done this before." would allow Him the freedom to reply, "I just want to be with you." Other things in life are equally as unnerving and unsettling.

It is the same with our experiences of death and dying. People have a hard time being around the dying and those grieving a recent death. We squirm for what to do and say. We are uncomfortable. Perhaps we need to learn how to plug into the discomfort of the situation, acknowledge it, and see what happens after that.

Simply saying to the dying and grieving, "This is really uncomfortable because I do not know what to do or say" would allow them the freedom to say, "I just want someone to be with me."

Silence and stillness are both very powerful images of death. It is no wonder we are unnerved and unsettled in their presence. The Fathers of the desert made no bones about it, most of them counseled for ascetics to keep their own death before their eyes—all day long. Not only was it meant to be a humble reminder of our impermanence and material weakness, it was a reminder that in Christ, we are all to have died. We are no longer alive, but Christ in us.

Silence and stillness are mirrors of death. Without an open acknowledgement of our fears we cannot be set free to learn to simply be with God, others, and ourselves. We will mirror our fears in all we do, if we do not wrestle with these fears. If we do not learn ways to create new associations and build new pathways we will never mirror anything beyond these initial fears.

Another way we can become comfortable with silence and stillness is taking them in measured doses. While we are in our cairn-space, after we have performed some sort of practice, we should sit quiet and still for two minutes at first. Then we can bump it up to four minutes.

Slowly increasing our exposure to silence will help us become familiar with the space it creates. In this way we are increasing the frequency of success and the building of positive neural pathways. We are also limiting the amount of time that logosmoi have to emerge. This will help us in the long run to become better at dealing with them one at a time and returning to the "slowing" of our lives, our true scope.

Another piece of silence that bothers us is having to deal with the things that flow out of our hearts and minds. When we sit in stillness there is a lot of time and space to reflexively analyze our own life—analyze what emerges from the depths. We often sense things we do not like.

We overhear ourselves saying things we cannot tolerate. We notice we are feeling things that seem inappropriate. We do not like what we sense and we recoil. We feel that leaving the silence and stillness will make everything go away.

We think stopping our quiet time will destroy what we have sensed. It simply removes the projection of the inner reality. The reality stays the same. That thing we sensed will be there the next time we return to stillness.

This is why we try to trace our arisings to their root. We are going to the beginning of the neural pathway. We return to our practice in hopes of building a new pathway. We are learning that we can make it through this without having to give up altogether. We simply find out what is really arising in us and begin again.

This ability to overhear our own self—our own story—is a unique feature to humanity. With the development of the neo-cortex in the human species comes the development of reflexive thought. We are able to think back on ourselves. We can perceive our own sense of self among the landscape of life—both our exterior and our interior self.

This radical shift in brain hardware is what prompts people to say that we are the consciousness of God. Our ability to reflect and review places us in a completely different category in the realm of the created.

Without the human ability to reflect back on our placement in this world of wonder and awe, there is no one here to say "I adore You for Your mighty deeds of love and creation." Jesus knew that the rocks could cry out, if we chose not to call out to God from the depths of our being. Our role in this cosmic dance is to make things conscious. This is what we are doing in silence and stillness. We are watching and becoming aware of all that arises; much like watching creation. When it arises, we identify it, where it came from, and then return to our practice.

The antidote for anguishing arisings that occur in our hearts and minds is acknowledging their existence and seeing what they are connected to. We then entrain them into a more healthy response by returning to our prayer practice.

If I am sitting down to pray and am about to enter into stillness and a thought arises, "I hate Joe", then I should not get up and leave my prayer-closet because I have failed to live a life of love. I should trace it to its root. "I hate Joe because he embarrassed me in front of my friends." Then I return to my prayer practice so I can re-center myself. We do not judge what arises, because judging is just another attempt to side track us from dealing with the issue by acknowledging its presence and its root.

Jesus encouraged us to retrain these thoughts by going to our brother and repairing the relationship. He asked us to replace the hatred with a new pathway: a pathway of love and forgiveness. This outward retraining of emotion and behavior is connected to the inner practice of merging our arisings with our spiritual practice. One mirrors the other.

Judging sets up a whole separate mutant topic in our hearts and minds, "It is bad that I have done this." Then from that place we move on to feeling guilt and shame over the event. Tracing arisings to their root, identifying where they are connected to us and then reestablishing a positive practice will help us to fire healthy neural communications that will not swallow us in their complex tentacles. This is watchfulness. This is guarding the heart.

If there is an image for the process of silence and stillness in the spiritual journey. It is a movement out and away from the darkness of void. Something emerging from the great expanse of nothing. The image is the expansion of reality to visible proportions. The desolate places make a perfect geographical ally for this vision.

We can allow ourselves to shorten our stillness and return to the practice. We can become still again. This next time for a little longer. Returning to the practice and increasing our stillness again. Slowly we learn to habitualize our comfort with the silent stillness of the Father.

Skellig Michael (Michael's rock) is an island on which a Celtic monastic community was founded in the seventh century, AD. The remoteness and barrenness of the island—seven miles out at sea—are a living physical definition of silence and stillness.

For six hundred years, Celtic monks lived in clochans (stone beehive shaped huts) nestled above the cliff walls of the island. They were 714 feet above sea level. Like most Celtic monks, they endured the austere ruggedness required of island life. They saw it as an image of the true arena for the spiritual athlete. Battling the monstrous forces of the Norseman was one of the many hardships they faced. Weather was another. Obtaining food yet another. They always battled the stillness and the silence.

The spiritual journey is not easy. The Celtic monks did not shy away from difficulty. They knew it was a battle until the end.

There is some resonance here for the one who battles with the sacred cairns of silence and stillness. If you believe the spiritual life should be easy, you will probably not accept the connection of the pious life with the image of Skellig Michael. If you understand the call of the monks on Skellig Michael, you will probably be willing to give "hesychia" a go.

Perched in the open heat of the Atlantic Ocean, Irish monks—Saint Patrick himself—were said to have done battle with serpents and dragons. It is told that the Archangel Saint Michael joined up with Patrick on the island to aid in the struggle; putting an end to the enemy. Hence the name: Michael's Rock.

The lore of snakes and demons are beyond commonplace in the lives of the early Christian monks both here and in the deserts. The imaginations of the heart and mind that crawl out of the cairns of silence and stillness are no less snakes and demons than the ones the monks battled long ago. Anyone attempting to sit quietly knows this.

I often wonder if it is the Adversary we are battling within our lives; or, if we are battling against the call of opportunity from the Holy Spirit. Sure, the Adversary may be the one tempting us into following the mutant trail of arisings in our prayer life, but perhaps these arisings have been allowed by God to give us opportunities to grow. Maybe this is the meaning behind the story of Job. We always have a choice of how we respond to the things that arise in life. How we respond will surely change the neural hardwiring of how we receive life's arisings in the future.

The image of desolation and isolation is the image of death, silence, stillness, the desert, the Skelligs, Mount Athos, and ultimately the image of the human heart. It is the great place of being alone with the Alone. This is why the spiritual journey is taken up in the desert and the remote places. It is in these places that we discover an energy that is most often left untapped—an energy that is below the surface. People have always known the desert and desolate places to be a cairn for the spiritual life.

The fear of unleashing the mighty powers from Pandora's box is clearly at the root of why the desert energy is left untapped. We fear we may not be able to control whatever it is that emerges. This is an underlying fear of the spiritual life—we may lose everything. We may unleash a force that will overpower us and take everything from us. This fear becomes a reality in the spiritual journey. Entering the heart is entering the center of a mass confluence of forces. Entering the heart is entering the eye of the storm.

There is a quote from the Gnostic Gospel of Thomas that speaks to this fear. It tells us that if we bring forth that which is within us, what we bring forth will save us. But, if we do not bring forth that which is within us, that which we do not bring forth will destroy us (vs. 70).

We must give passage to the arisings in our hearts and minds. We give passage by acknowledging that they have come forth from within us. We return to our practice to align ourselves with health. The stuff that is coming out of us is coming out of us for a reason. Hiding it or hiding from it is not the answer.

We forget that behind the angels, and demons, and Adversary of the desert is the LORD of all. The Supreme God of life. No demon, or Adversary, or angel for that matter, gains access to us unless God allows this. The things that emerge are known to the Father of Lights. If they come forth, it is so we may be free of them.

We are ultimately asked to yield and surrender to the force from the desert. This force, which is in fact not the Adversary as had we expected, but God Himself, is using the Adversary to purify us. The angels and demons must be brought forth so we may attain to God.

The goal of the spiritual life is hidden in this power of yielding to God. Bonhoeffer alluded to this when he said, "When Christ calls a man, He bids him come and die." (Cost of Discipleship). We are to die to our preconceived notions of our self. We must die to the old self. We must die in the purification of the heart.

In cold-war America, the deserts were turned into testing grounds for nuclear devices. Men ran into the sand to test their ability to destroy everything. They unleashed the Armageddon potentiality hidden in the atoms of life. Trampling down all life with death. Immense forces are unleashed in the desert. That means we were unleashing an awesome power toward destruction into our hearts. These were perilous times.

It would appear there is some archetypal acknowledgement that the solitude of the desert is charged with energy, filled with power. Thomas Merton pointed this out to us wonderfully in his book "Thoughts in Solitude." There is a power in the wilderness of the heart that is greater than we can imagine. The heart is the eye of the storm.

The desert calls us into life on the edge—on the edge of living and dying. God, man, angels, the Adversary, and demons are all in the desert. A place God goes to meet man. A place man goes to meet God. It is a place for which most men have found no use. Except for the ascetics. Except for the "world-destroyers" (reference Oppenheimer's quote: "Now I am become Death, the destroyer of worlds."—Bhagavad Gita). The desert is the heart. The heart is the eye of the storm.

Life in the desert is the ultimate grazing place for the ravenous spirit of man and the demons. One may not go into the desert with matted hair and a grizzled appearance. One surely finds them there.

The desert is the great equalizer. All mountains are brought down low, all valleys are filled-in. This is the experience of raw encounter and wrestling with the Divine. God changes us in the desert, even if the desert is a small place in the home and in the heart of the believer. Power, great power is in the desert of the human heart.

What is produced in the desert is a crystallized form of humanity. The surplus of life is boiled away in the encounter and wrestling of the monastic with God. When we analyze the literature that comes from the throngs at Sketis and Nitria we find a body of literature that resembles the haiku or koan. Their words are concise. What they teach us is the ability to reduce things to manageable sizes. Massive concepts and theories are reduced to truncated statements and actions.

The sayings attributed to the Mothers and Fathers of the desert— in the Apophthegmata Patrum—are small in size but mighty in stature. They reveal what is possible for humanity when it removes all barriers to thought-action. When we remove all of the extra words about God, we are left with powerful doses of Divine Meetings. These meetings change us deeply. These meetings are cairns in the desert.

These sayings contain an immense number of references to wrestling with God, angels, and demons. There is something about the desert, about the distillation of the process of the heart, that lends itself to wrestling. Jesus did the same when He was in the Desert. Whether God, or angels, or demons, or the Satan, the power we find in the desert is conflictual at best. It stimulates wrestling encounters. This is another reason it is hard to sit with silence and stillness—we start wrestling. We are battling for our lives, many times.

The desert experience is about the stripping away of everything that is not spiritual. Because of this barrenness, there is time and space for the angels and demons of our personalities to emerge and battle for our attention. When we live in the Empire, the consumerism and bureaucracy of the landscape repels the inner battle and numbs us from feeling the conflicts of being human.

We struggle to make a go of it in the arena of survival and exchange of goods and services. We can find many things to distract us from the battle to purify our souls. Without the distraction, the heart opens up and reveals what is really hidden within it.

We can expect nothing less when we enter the cave of our heart. We may find solace and unity as we begin the work. But, at some point the cell, prayer closet, and heart will become a refiners fire. We will long to flee it, run for the city, and hide from the processes of isolation: purification, enlightenment, and union. Many do not survive the power of the desert and leave it, or die in its heat.

There is ample speculation about what the monks of Skellig Michael ate. Some say they tilled the rocky soil, some say they raised rabbits, others say they ate fish, seaweed, and bird eggs. I would venture a guess that the "pragmatic monk" (should there have been one on the island) ate whatever was available—whenever it was available. They ate whatever arose.

Look at our biblical narratives about feeding in the desert. Moses and the Israelites ate manna from heaven. Elijah the Tishbite at food dropped off by God's ravens. Jesus was given the chance to eat stones, John ate locust and honey. Pragmatic.

The work of the heart produces food for the journey. It may not be a sumptuous feast. It may be food that spoils if it is kept in jars for more than a day. The heart produces food; something always arises. Pragmatic.

I remember a powerful story emerging from one of my days of sitting at the cairn of my heart. Memories of my childhood and being left alone in the upstairs to sleep without anyone else up there arose and littered my vista. I remembered the crying out I did for someone to come and sit with me. What a feast that was. My heart gave voice to the depths of my soul: we all long for companionship—even God. I learned to acknowledge the aloneness I had felt as a child.

It took me a while to come to see this experience as nourishing, but in the end it became the fuel that enabled me to live through experiences of isolation, hoping for the redemption of community. It gave me eyes to see and ears to hear the cry of the poor and abandoned. We all long for companionship.

This is the kind of grist that is milled in the heart. This is what we walk away from the desert learning and knowing. These morsels are not always happy thoughts, but they are nourishment for the journey. These are the notions that enable us to understand the call of evangelism.

Evangelism is about helping people address the aloneness of human life. Evangelism exists somewhere between the notion that God is with us, and that when Jesus was alone and in prison we visited Him.

We have to learn to eat what arises.

There are many practices we can engage in our cairn-space. As we first sit to settle and focus ourselves, we should look to do something that will point us into the silence and stillness with some direction.

I have already mentioned simple prayers, prayer services, or the Psalms. The words of these venues give our heart something to latch onto as we enter the stillness of "hesychia." If we are reading a Psalm, it may say something about "hiding in the shadow of His wings." This thought and feeling become a natural image to hold onto as we experience the stillness. We may sense ourselves hidden in God. We may long for the feeling of being held.

There are other practices as well. We can write in a journal and read back what we have written. Then we can sit with the residue of those words. We can read a scripture over and over; listening for the words that jump out at us and speak to us (lectio divina). We may try visualizations—reading a portion of the Gospel stories and inserting ourselves as one or all of the characters.

The key is that we do the practice and then sit with the residues left with us, trusting the Spirit to do a good work in us. Ultimately, the Fathers felt that we should move from this form of imaging and imagination to the utter emptiness of meeting God without image and without word. But, this is a process on a continuum. We must first be able to regulate our stillness through the use of images and imagination.

These radical experiences of emptiness and quiet stillness are experiences that defy the beginner and are surely not something we will encounter for some time. They are gifts that we will be given when we put ourselves to the regular task of wrestling. So at first, we should hold on to something we have taken from our practice.

We may imagine ourselves as the one who gathered all he had and sold it so he could buy a field that held a single pearl of great price. We may visualize ourselves as the woman with an issue of blood that reached through the crowd to touch the hem of Christ's garment. We may offer ourselves as Simon of Cyrene, shouldering the cross for our Jesus as he walked to Golgotha. Wrestling. Wrestling. Wrestling.

We should have some imagining to hold on to. When the arisings come we go back to the practice. The arisings may take the form of a thought that says, "You don't need to buy the field, you can just visit it." Return to the practice. The arisings may take the form of a thought that says, "You're not as bad off as the woman with an issue of blood." Return to the practice. Whatever comes forth to distract you from sitting in stillness with the residue of your practice, acknowledge it, and return to your practice.

What is happening in the process of practice and stillness is that we are using images to settle us. We notice an arising and we return to the simple prayer practice that we have begun. Regardless of the practice, the prayers we offer are filled with images that our mind and heart will connect to. This will help us refocus in order to settle down. It will rebuild a path into the stillness of the neural desert.

If we pray a Psalm, our mind will create snapshots of the things in the Psalm that we are reading—images—and we will settle into these. For example if we pray, "As the deer pants for water, so my soul pants for You" (Psalm, xlii, 1), we will make an interior image of a thirsty deer and visually connect it with ourselves. Then we approach the stillness with the residue of this image. An arising of thought or emotion may try to lead us off the trail, and so we acknowledge it and we return to our practice and create another focusing image.

In this way we move from imaging to imagelessness. It takes time, but this is the pattern. The heart and the mind work together in the process. The repetition of the process is actually hardwiring the practice into our neural pathways.

The mind often creates the interior image and the heart attaches feeling and impressions to that image. Eventually the heart and mind will cease needing images to settle into silent stillness.

Most of the monks of the desert or island cairn-space tended to go the journey alone. They still submitted their hearts to an elder for correction. They spoke about what they discovered in their heart with another cairn-builder. This was purposeful.

The intention behind sharing our heart-stuff is having someone else preview the inner process with us. We may begin to feel proud because of our experiences. The fellow journeyman will tell us to be careful of pride. We may find despair or loneliness in the pilgrimage. The fellow journeyman will tell us to be strong and of good cheer. We would go mad if we did not submit our inner process to the community of cairn-builders.

It is a good idea to have a group to share experiences with. This is perhaps the greatest call before the modern Church. Can we produce small "gatherings" ("ekklesia")—that can be therapeutic communities administering the medicine of the Spirit? Can we grow communities of vulnerable togetherness before God? Can the Church learn the lost art of therapy?

The stories from the "Sayings of the Fathers" remind us of the value of shared experience. In them, we find examples that the shared cairn-experience produces fruit in many, not just one.

The story was shared about Abba Isidore that one day he went to the market to sell the baskets he had made. As he approached the market, anger welled up inside him. He told the journey-folk that he dropped everything and fled because of the anger. He felt all his work had come undone. His distress got the better of him and the distraction of failure won out.

Without the sharing of these tales, the journey-folk would not have seen the value of the struggle. Abba Isidore was reminding them that all we work for could perish in an instant. We could lose all we have established in us; it is possible. He lost hope because of what arose, but he shared this openly so others could learn from his hopelessness. This is why we must collaborate on the journey. Go into the Alone, but bring that experience back to the community.

Abba Isidore is also reminding us that the experiences of the heart do not cinch things up for good. Having heart experiences does not mean we are perfect. Sanctification (or "theosis" in the Eastern Church) is a process, not an event.

We must approach the heart everyday and listen for that day's wealth, for that day's arisings. The manna in the wilderness molded if the Jews tried to hoard it for another day's food. There was no stockpiling of manna. So too, there is no stockpiling of cairn-experience. We go it anew, each and everyday. We have the neural circuitry to enhance the travel, but we must start anew each day.

You would be mistaken to believe that the words here in this book will give you a solid platform on which to stand for the rest of your days. There is one thing that can do that, that is the One. We must approach Him afresh at every opportunity. Like the man who said that he would tear down his barns to build bigger ones to store more for the future; our lives may be required of us this night. Burn down your barns in your mind before you go to sleep.

Give us this day our daily manna. Pragmatic cairn-builders eat whatever is available, when it is available. This is the wisdom of insecurity for our current age of anxiety.

∾ ∾ ∾

"THE CRUMBS"

The crumbs I found
in my heart today
will feed me.
I will eat
only one, until
the sun is high.
Then,
I will gather
with the others
who have come
to this place
looking for manna,
and locust,
and raven's food.
A morsel
can feed many,
obliging itself
to multiplication
inside
filling the soul
like a sated stomach
only to be
hungry tomorrow.
The sight of
a new iris
only holds my wonder
for an hour,
maybe two.
A powerful wind
can shake my awe
for the same.
These crumbs,
I will save
to feed many

that we
may gather up
baskets of meaning –
overflowing
all expectation,
giving sup
to those beyond our
place in
the sand.

Chapter Six

Those things that the monks were building in the isolated communities of Nitria, Sketis, Kellia, and Skellig Michael were not just waddles of daub or stone; they were environments of pious living and holy air. Those geologic caves were not just shelters, but spiritual spaces. They needed to hallow the present. They sought to deify time and place. They brought God down to earth by allowing Him tabernacle in their hearts. They brought earth to heaven, by opening the desert to the Divine Milieu.

When we put forth the material that is within, we are creating reality. Our interior milieu attaches itself to and manipulates the material world. It is fashioned into the life we live and radiates out onto the world and others. What we think fills the air around us. What we feel permeates space with its energy. The nature of our heart impacts the measure of our days. Our sense of core values influences our schedules.

When we hold angst and terror in our hearts and minds we make a world around us that is unsure and bitter. When we hold awe and wonder in our hearts and minds we create a world of radical amazement and peace. Placing stones on the cairn of life's edifice is what we do with every hope, dream, desire, and whim. Recognizing that this is what we are doing, and then taking conscious control of that process is a major step in the human odyssey.

When we hold anger in our heart toward someone, it creates a relationship that is fraught with discord. No matter what we do with that person, it will be based on, and permeated with some seeds of that anger. If we are pretending not to be angry, it will be based on and permeated with some seeds of deceit as well.

This is why the ascetics strove to allow the angels and demons of the Godly life to emerge and to cut off everything that was not good and holy by returning to their practice of prayer. They watched and waited to see what lie at the root of every thought, action, desire, and emotion. They submitted what came out of them to the rule of scripture and holy living and did away with all things that were not Christ. They refashioned their arisings by retraining the pathway of their thoughts. They created new neural pathways.

The nature of the life we live is intertwined with what we posit forth and project outward. We really do have control over where we are going. Life is built one mystic brick at a time. Choosing which bricks we toss aside and which bricks we build with is what we are trying to accomplish in the desert stillness of our interior cell and cave. Our hearts are a proving ground, if you will.

I am reminded of Saint Francis in Zeffirelli's 1972 movie "Brother Sun and Sister Moon." He often breaks out into 1960's and 70's song and lyric via the voice of Donovan. It is seemingly appropriate for this minstrel of joy. This odyssey of the Franciscan journey aligns perfectly with the freedom from attachment that the hippie movement strove to attain.

One of the most memorable songs from the show boasts: "If you want your dreams to be, take your time go slowly. Small beginnings greater ends, heartfelt work is holy. Day by day, stone by stone, build your secret slowly. Day by day, you'll grow too. You'll see heavens glory." This is how it is done. One stone at a time. Before you know it, you have a full-blown edifice.

"FRANCIS"

I remember your eyes.
The way they softly
unfolded the chains
wrapped around the hearts
of so many.
How your bare
hands and feet
touched the earth,
touched the stones
and rebuilt God's
Church.
It was Damiano's
at first,
then,
slowly

among the hills
and dales
all across Europe,
piles of stones were
raised to house
simple beings of
love and prayer.
Never asking
for more than the
day's needs,
your beggars wandered
the earth and stones
looking for places
to pray –
to open
their poor,
simple hearts to God.
All of the saints
and
all of the angels
can not compare
to one simple soul
that seeks out shelter
in the heart—crying
desperately to God
who longs to hear.
One stone,
one soul,
one heart at a time;
God builds and rebuilds
His Church.
Where have you gone
Francis,
where is your spirit
of freedom from
attachment today?
Our Church needs you
to throw away all

of our possessions.
We have become addicted
to what we own and
what we can add to
our list of acquisitions.
We have forgotten
to acquire the Holy Spirit.
We no longer hunger
to be joyful,
humble,
and simple.
Return to us, brother of
the heart. Come back to
us simple man of Assisi.
We need to know how
to give up everything
to follow the heart of
Jesus.

~ ~ ~

Donovan's song is exactly what we are getting at in our discussion. We are building a building slowly over time. The quality and tenor of the cell that we are building—this ambiance that we carry about with us—is up to us to fashion.

Shall we build a cell of compassion and grace or shall we build a cell of enmity and sterility. Shall we build a heart of moral platitudes or shall we build a heart of compassion and grace. What we build inside of us—what we carry around in us—is reflected on the walls of our exterior life and takes on three dimensional reality in our interactions and activities. Our inner cell is visible all around us.

It is most often our nature to collect, purchase, and arrange "stuff" all around us. Actual physical "stuff", like baskets, mementos, pictures, and gadgets. We like to gather "things" into our lives.

This hunger for acquisition is a very real thing in the life of a human. It is a hungering for wholeness. It is an acknowledgement of our connection to form and to something "other" than us. I fear, though, that we too often allow the buying of "chachka" and "baubles" (to put out on our shelves) to fulfill this hunger for completion. We do not often trace the hunger to its root and acknowledge that we long for a completion that no on "thing" can assuage.

Is that what we were created for? Are we nothing more than individual gift-shop builders? Does God wish us to collect little trinkets and trophies from our wanderings on earth? Are we in the business of mergers and acquisitions? If we are, how shall we get them to the other side?

As we each do our building of interior cairn-space, we are joined in a fanfare of construction by the building plans of every other person we each come into contact with. The mirroring neurons are very perceptive. The one who offers us water, causes us to build gently and with thanks. The one who curses us, begs us to realign our simple love into protective weariness and suspicion. The one who threatens us makes us paralyzed and unsure.

So, we build. Most often we are not aware that we are fashioning whole metropolises of thought and emotion all around us. These cities often have not become freeing empires but prisons of despair and entrapment. Imagine what kind of invisible structures hate and animosity make. How they would feel desperate and agonizing. Then imagine how inviting and alluring the air would be around someone who is always creating love in their lives—glorious palaces of compassion.

Have you ever noticed how when one thing goes wrong it can trigger a chain reaction? Everything we touch from that point on seems to be tainted with the aftershock of the first problem. We tell ourselves that things happen in "threes" so we don't get overwhelmed by the possibility that our distraction at the first conflict has set in motion a series of similar conflicts that will go on forever. We allow and tolerate decline because we hold the thought in us that this is the way it will be.

We often stay the same because we are tangled in webs of addiction to ways of believing, feeling, speaking, hoping, and remembering. We do not move beyond these places because we are tied to them and their streets are winding mazes of despair. We are comfortable in the familiarity of the landscape. Cutting off these hopeless images of being tied to failures is as simple as dealing with all arisings. Acknowledge them and return to the practice.

We are always inaugurating the development of the immediate environment around us by how we carry ourselves within. Jesus called us to rid ourselves of holding onto murderous thoughts. The presence of these thoughts changes who we are. Our heart becomes numb. It is as if we actually committed the act itself. I believe He was leading us to streams of wisdom; teaching us that the thoughts and feelings we harbor deep inside shape our personalities and the very spaces we inhabit. As a man thinks, so he is.

We all know how repelling grumpy people are. We have all dodged the church "gossip" because we feel dark and corrupt having listened to his stinging verbal barbs and cuts. We all sense when something is a bit askew.

What shapes the air around us—around all beings—is the intention of the heart. What we (and they) allow ourselves to hold inside is what we create outside as well. If we notice bitterness and do not trace its root and seek its antidote by acknowledging it and returning to the practice, then it stays in us and projects onto our surroundings.

Think of the mirroring neurons. We may not recognize how, but the things inside of us stay within us and radiate outside us just the same. We must learn the skill of cutting off thoughts, feelings, impressions and desires that are harmful to ourselves and our communities.

This process of arising does not only occur in our spiritual practices. They can arise in our dealings with other people as well. We apply the same antidote to our wakeful active life. We trace these things to their root and we retrain our neural circuitry toward the wholesome, toward the good.

The prospects of doing battle with the things that emerge from the silence of the desert hut or the cave of the heart is daunting at best. This is what the spiritual practices were developed for. The ascetics developed weapons to defend themselves from the onslaught of demons and false gods that emerged in their lives. They not only cut down the abhorrent things they saw, they replaced them with holy things. They had antidotes to the diseases they discovered within themselves.

The clear reminder from the Gnostic Gospel of Thomas (70) was something the desert saints understood. Bring forth that which is within you so it does not kill you. You can rush through life and hide the interior machinations of the heart, but in the end, they will be your demise.

We must first commit ourselves to making a space and the time to allow these things to emerge. When they do emerge, we must cut of the unhealthy things, further establish the healthy things, applying antidotes to nurse ourselves to fuller health. This is the process of encounter and wrestling. It is the process of true prayer and spirituality.

We have too long believed the spiritual life was a rattling off of shopping lists to God; simply learning rules cognitively, and rendering superficial praises for all of the things that worked out just so nicely for us. The spiritual life may begin at this place, but it needs a deepening. We must move from drinking only milk for nourishment, to eating a substantive meat. Going deeper feeds us meat.

Paradigms are shifting all over the world. We are in a deep questioning phase in the life of humans on the planet. The implications are not just environmental, social, political, and technological, they are spiritual as well. We have believed for too long that programs, organizations, and empires could be responsible for spiritual growth and development.

What place does the spiritual athlete find in church meetings and programmatic campaigns? Is their space for people to encounter and wrestle the demons and angels in them? Are there specific manifestations of angels and demons that groups of believers face when they are together? Do sermons and worship venues offer true transformation and healing of the sickness of the soul that we find in us when we do not tend the garden? Do any of the habits of "Church" (that we have wrapped with the myelin sheaths of repetition) offer life? Are the routines of "modern Church" simply things we have not thought out, or have the behaviors we have learned turned into prisons from which we cannot escape?

It seems "Church" has been hijacked. Our identity has been stolen.

The effects of what we harbor inside, over time, reveal themselves in the structure of the communities we build and inhabit. It is no wonder that homes, churches, neighborhoods, and businesses that are filled with people of angst and duplicity fail because of hopelessness and deceit. These attributes have been planted in the garden, watered, and they have come to fruition. They are built one stone at a time. The stones may be fetid or firm, but we build gradually with each stone. What we build into something is what remains present.

Look around you. What is the nature of your building? How do you interact with others? What odor exudes from the pores of your life? Are your interactions reflections of the encountering and wrestling that you do with the Holy One? Do you and your "Far Mosque" emanate a sense of the Holy, the scriptures, and the rule of life? Do you create palaces of dung and stubble? What are the quality and texture of the stones with which you are building? What do people come to expect from you?

The retreat house where we live offers a day apart three times a year for clergy. We have offered it for almost two years. The number of clergy that actually attend this day is minimal. We have had under a dozen attendees in total since we began this offering.

The day is free. There is no structure. Folks can come up in the morning, hang out and seek the LORD until the end of the work day. We offer a free lunch of homemade soup, bread, salad and an entrée. We provide a bookshelf of materials for prayer and spiritual development to use while here. We have 750 acres of woodlands to wander. We designate a space in one of the lodges for participants of the retreat.

The lack of participation is sad to me. I think we have allowed the job of the clergy to become so filled with the activities necessary to run the business side of the church, that they do not feel comfortable taking time to just crash and seek God. Many clergy have abandoned the pathways of spiritual development that they were on because they are just too busy. They are no longer engaged in the ministry they were called to.

What does this say about the current state and nature of the Church? It does not take a lot of time to "Google" and find surveys on the spiritual lives of clergy. Most find themselves in a position of not offering any ongoing spiritual formation in their churches. Many only read the scriptures in preparation for their Sunday homilies. Most find little time to pray.

This is not right. If this is the state of the clergy, how difficult must it be for lay people to pursue an active spiritual formation and direction in their lives? If the clergy are sending out these deficiencies into the world around them as neural communications, how can the lay folk not mirror these deficiencies in kind?

It takes a strong heart, mind, soul, and spirit to approach God regularly in a spiritual practice. It is difficult to wrestle with God, angels, and demons. It takes devotion to maintain an ongoing connectedness to the Father of Lights and His kingdom of brightness. It requires building our interior edifice of spiritual formation and direction one stone at a time —over time. Over a long time.

Many people claim they do not have the time. I do not think time is the real reason people do not attempt the work. I believe it is difficult work. We are having to look deeply into ourselves and we often can not stand what we discover. We are having to make changes in ourselves; cutting out the dead portions of our lives and cultivating the living portions.

This means stopping ourselves from all of the negative activity that builds interior palaces of pride and anger. This means learning new ways to build love, mercy, and forgiveness into our interior cells and reflect them in the world around us. It means approaching death, grief, silence, and stillness. It means entering the heart. The heart is the eye of the storm.

This is difficult work. Abba Moses was allegedly said to have asked Abba Sylvanus if a man could make a new beginning—lay a new foundation—everyday. Sylvanus told him that with hard work, he could begin again every moment. Building cairn-pace is not something we can do half heartedly; we build it every moment.

Many of the desert acetic athletes taught that the cure of the soul could only begin when we looked to lighten the darkened mind and purify the impure heart. This requires a watchfulness that can eventually enable us to identify and cut off negative influences that can easily run our lives. This requires entering into the paradise of Eden that we left long ago. Paradise is still available to us. The garden is the place of our true identity.

The Nag Hammadi library contains a book called "The Thunder, Perfect Mind." The text is from the Sophia tradition of biblical pseudopygrapha. It contains a series of aphoristic statements that offer a thesis and an antithesis. The piece poises our mind in the middle between the conjunctions of these pairs of opposites—the place of wisdom. It claims that the kingdoms are within the mind. That is both heaven and hell—thesis and antithesis. It cautions us to guard ourselves and choose wisely which kingdom we will espouse, which kingdom we will enact.

The "Tanya"—an 18th century Jewish text at the heart of the Chabad Hasidim —begins with the notion that wrestling with opposites is vital for the journey. Every Jew is told—before they leave heaven to come to earth—to be righteous and not wicked. Even if everyone on earth views you as righteous, you should maintain yourself as wicked in your own mind. The text poises our mind in between a pair of opposites.

The tension between poles is critical on the Royal Road. It tends to elicit the process of movement toward wisdom. It is an instigator of the wrestling process.

Without wrestling there is no life. The Garden is attainable. But the Garden is guarded by an angel with a fiery sword. You must wrestle to get in.

Poles of opposites exist for us to discriminate between. We are meant to be beings of choice. When we do not choose (which as we know is a choice itself) we are creating worlds we may not wish to inhabit.

Abba Evagrios, in his texts on "Discrimination", suggests that there are three demons we must wrestle with at the beginning of our spiritual journey. These three assail us throughout the work we do to create cairn-space. The demons are gluttony (that passion for consuming food and sexuality), avarice thoughts (the desire for more than we have), and vainglory or the esteem of other men (the longing for acknowledgement and power). These three are woven into our path in often subtle ways.

Lists like this one are not hard to come by in the ascetic tradition of Christianity. Abba Evagrios goes on to list a total of eight demons or vices. If any progress is to be made in the purification of the heart, then these demons must be wrestled with over and over again. The full list of demons from Evagrios' "Praktikos" is: gluttony, luxury, avarice, anger, sadness, accedia, vainglory and pride. Abba John Cassian and Gregory the Great wrote out the list again, only their lists held that pride was the root of the other seven vices; so their lists of vices contain seven and not eight vices.

It is safe to say that regardless of the practice we put in place to clear the way into the presence of God in cairn-space, that we will do battle with these illnesses as we sit in silence listening for the voice of God in our heart. The Neptic Fathers (as they are often called; "nepsis" meaning "watchfulness") taught that our stillness and silence would be invaded by these demons. They would try to throw us off the scent of tracking down the Holy One.

The writings of the desert ascetics were meant to be a guide to-ward dismantling these sicknesses and unhealthy structures within our heart. If we apply their words, like a salve or balm, we will find healing and be able to move through the silence and stillness from the battle of the imagination to a passion for God that is not hampered by images from the imagination. We will move beyond the things that arise to distract us.

It is not uncommon for us to imagine—during our times of cairn-space—that we are somehow better than others. We should receive praise for our hard work. This sense of vainglory or esteem from others is something we must confront. If we do not, we will perish on the vine.

This is why people feel at a loss for wanting to continue the spiritual journey. We uncover dark and sinister desires in us that we do not know what to do with. The remedy for this illness—the antidote—is acknowledging "the arisings" and a return to our simple prayer practice.

We will begin to gain a fuller awareness of the name and nature of the things arising in us as time goes by. We will become familiar with the terrain. When we do, it is helpful to tailor the simple prayer practice to include specific scriptures, prayers, and writings of the desert monks to "dash" (ascetic terminology that may be better understood as "realign") these thought forms that arise.

The more familiar we become with our "arisings" (angels and demons), the more likely we will be able to select the appropriate antidote to retrain our pathways toward stillness. Repetition will help us to gain access to a cure.

We wait, we watch, and we "battle" (realign) each one until we are assailed no more. The "battling" is simply about acknowledging what arises and returning to the practice so we may move closer to stillness.

The military/athletic language is very prevalent in monastic literature. Battling, wrestling, and dashing are simply terms meant to identify a deeply strenuous process is going on. When we are able to realign the arisings, we will be moving from purification to enlightenment.

When lust arises, we "smash" it by reminding ourselves that our flesh withers like the grass, a verse from the Psalms. The Fathers also encouraged monks to visit graves and notice how fleeting this physical attraction was. They believed this image would "retrain" their hearts and minds.

When we feel pride arise in us, we are counseled to remember that we are only doing what we were asked to do by the LORD (become perfect as our Father in Heaven is perfect) nothing more. This is no great feat. Verses from the Proverbs can be a sure remedy to our wandering demons of pride, as well. The verses help to settle the imagery, and to return us to our practice so we may approach stillness.

Many faithful followers are derailed at this early stage and never return to the practice of approaching God in sacred space. They feel like they should be able to do battle once and then be done with that demon. This is not the case.

These demons assail us our whole life. The spiritual journey is not easy, it is a constant battle. In a day and age when we expect immediate answers to our issues, we are at a loss for what to feel and how to respond in this kind of situation.

We lack tenacity. There is no linear order to the work, there is no checklist for accomplishments. The list of vices is simply the beginning of what we may encounter on the inner terrain. It is not exhaustive. Each day is anew and each sitting is a battle all its own.

We must keep a daily feeding of scripture, the sayings of the desert monks, and other spiritual practices in our lives if we expect to win the battle. We cry out to God for help, but we use these tools as specific guides for receiving that help from above.

The challenge for the Church is to encourage the clergy to do spiritual battle within themselves so they may edify the saints of God and not just simply prepare for finance meetings and strategic planning. We should not have them running corporate board meetings, but "battling" the angels, the demons, and God Himself so they can speak a word of kindness to those on the journey.

If we allow our leaders to be bureaucrats then we will only build a bureaucracy. If we demand they become "Neptic Fathers and Mothers", then we build a Church that is modeled after the wise and watchful virgins of the Gospels. The virgins waited for the return of the Bridegroom and the lamps of their lives were trimmed and filled. They were ready to enter into the Bridal train—the Marriage of God and man. Can we rebuild the interior structure of the life of the Church? Do we care to?

A simple practice for the cairn-space we build is to read two Psalms and then sit in silence. Imagine that you are sitting on a bench, along a brook, and that Jesus is sitting with you. Just continue to bring your attention back to sitting with Jesus on the bench along the brook. Then sit there in silence, with no notice of anything else.

Do not force anything else to arise from within. If other images naturally arise, trace them to their root and bring yourself back to this image—over and over again.

Do this for a few minutes. Practice it over and over again. It is helping you to develop a sense of watchfulness. If other images arise spontaneously, trace them to their root and go back to your simple image of sitting with Jesus on the bench along the brook. Then enter the silence again.

If we cannot keep our attention on this image, then we will have a hard time discerning and following the things that arise from our heart (things like gluttony, avarice, and self-esteem). Practice it often, again and again.

Chapter Seven

I HIKED TO COLUM-CILLE again today. I sat there and offered two Psalms; a practice to build my prayer-space. I sat on my bench at Colum-Cille imagining Jesus to be with me on the hill. I sat on the bench overlooking the rocks and trees and lake that lay at the base of my vantage point.

Jesus was with me. My first practice was the Psalms. My second practice was imaging Jesus with me. I wandered into stillness.

Several moments of stillness arose. Several times my heart did not wander and think about the mosquitoes in my ear, or my lost set of work pants, or the thunder in the distance. When stillness was broken, I remembered my practice of imaging Jesus and I could settle again.

Practice begets moments of stillness. Moments of stillness are disturbed by arisings. We use a practice to deal with the arisings and return to the stillness. It is a continual work to attain stillness. It is a circle, not a line.

We go round and round. And, although it may seem like an endless frustration that is for naught, it is not. Every moment we spend in prayer-space changes us. We are transformed by the renewal of our mind (think neural pathways). We become new people.

What we see today as an arising of lust, listlessness, or arrogance in our prayer-space is an opportunity of "watchfulness" that will set us free in the future. Now we see it in the imagination of our prayer space. Later, we will begin to notice the same things arising in our conversations and dealings with people. We will see the demons and the angels in our habits on this earth-place.

As we learn to recognize and deal with these things in cairn-space now, we are setting a new routine in place that will help us live more Christ-like lives in every area of our existence. This practice is wrapping myelin sheaths around the ability to be watchful at all times.

We ourselves are the cairns of God. We are icons of the Holy One in time and space. As image and likeness, we are markers of remembrance (a Eucharist) pointing toward and "giving presence" to the Holy One. We are points of arrival and departure along the neural pathways of the memory of God. History becomes the myelin sheath. We are pockets of existence in eternity.

We must find a way to bring this eternalness into our existence. We must find a way to bring heaven and earth together in our lives. We must enable the "Unmanifest" to become manifest. In this way, we may begin to see that God's practice is to find stillness with us.

Theology becomes the set of beliefs that we arrange along the far edges of experience. Theology asks us to "go no further" than the last set of markers on the horizon. The mystic knows that theology is only meant to reflect existence. It cannot reflect being. This is the path of "wordless union."

Merton stretched the understanding of the monastic life to reveal the core of the monk's nature. In one of his poems (Merton, T. "The Collected Poems of Thomas Merton, London. 1978, p 201), he scrawls out the mystic edges of what it means to be a solitaire:

"We are exiles in the far end of solitude, living as listeners,

With hearts attending to the skies we cannot understand:

Waiting upon the first far drums of Christ the Conqueror,

Planted like sentinels upon the world's frontier."

Monks stand as markers on the far edge of belief. This also means that they stand as places of departure into the mystic experience. This is an experience that can only happen at the edge.

Anthony, Arsenios, Amoun, Pachomios, Evagrios and the whole desert crew, left the empire, stretched the boundaries of Christian belief into the desert, and asked believers to follow them to the edge.

Theology must meet mysticism if it is to be whole. They must meet on the edges of experience, the edges of reality, and the edges of God and man. Theology and mysticism must meet in phenomenology. They must meet in perception and in conception. Theology and mysticism must bring the Divine Milieu into our neural pathways.

From that place; that new cairn in the desert, the monks and ascetics asked believers to leap into an experience of the Holy One that would change the philosophic structure of the Church forever. The desert communities became places of departure into God not just the experience of God. They marked—in time and space—a shift in the consciousness of the body of believers Christ left behind to grow.

You get that sense when you read the Sayings of the Fathers. There is some "otherworldliness" to them that you just cannot put a finger on. Something is different. They are not just about belief, but about something fuller. They bespeak levels of experience that theology can only hint at. In the unfolding of their vignettes comes an opening of desert paradise. We see how the heart and the wilderness are the same place. Man inhabits both of them. Awareness of the process enhances our ability to move in and out of the heart and the desert. Our awareness, our conscious self-reflection makes us human.

The creation of cairns is an "intentional" act of entering into union with God. It is marking off space and time in order to encounter and wrestle with God. It is a marking off of space and time in order to remind us that this encounter and wrestling is possible. We are trying to practice a sense of "awareness" of what we are doing when we make cairn-space. It is important to understand the place of intention, of conscious awareness, and of the "will" if we are to go the full distance as human mystics and believers.

Mindfulness itself brings a sense of consciousness to the process of building sacred space and time. We can establish sacredness in time and space by intentionally setting out to make holiness present now; bringing heaven and earth together.

This notion of merging heaven and earth is not a new idea. It has its lineaments in many places along man's quest for God. It made itself known quite loudly in the teachings of the Hasidic masters of Judaism. It was a goal of their piety. They longed to be a space for God to dwell on earth. Israel Ben Eliezer—the Baal Shem Tov—(knower of the GOOD NAME) lived this life of union. He taught his disciples how to open to the Indwelling One.

In order to bring heaven and earth together, we must work with a conscious attention to how we are "being" in this space of life. Then we must intend ourselves to live better in that space. This is encountering and wrestling. It is consciously assenting to allowing God entrance into human existence. It is allowing transformation to occur as a result of this entrance.

Go to the place you have chosen as a prayer space. Go there often. Sit there and imagine yourself entering into an encounter and a wrestling with the Divine. This is what I mean by intentional—recognize what you are doing as what you are doing it. You are going into prayer to encounter and wrestle with God.

Instead of simply sitting with Jesus, imagine yourself now wrestling with the angel of the LORD. Again, this image will help us to draw our attention on watching. When our thoughts wander, we come back to the image. Practice. Stillness. Practice. Stillness.

This sounds odd in the daily routine of life. It is nonetheless a critical acknowledgement. After a dozen years of working with people grieving the loss of loved ones, I began to see some patterns emerge from the work in regard to mending and intention.

One of these patterns was that people who told themselves that they were doing certain things (praying, meditating, visiting the opera, going to church, listening to music, writing in a journal) in order to take care of themselves in the process of mending after loss, were able to feel as if they were "mending" or "taking care" of themselves. Others, who were performing the same tasks and routines, and who were not consciously telling themselves that they did them to mend felt as if they were not mending or taking care of themselves. Intention made a difference.

Because the people in the first group told themselves they were taking care of themselves, they were able to believe and feel that they actually were mending. Intention is the critical factor missing from most of what we do.

Intention makes all of the difference. Intention brings the fullness of our soul into the work. Intention offers our "will" to the process.

The pragmatic allure of physical existence leaves us feeling more comfortable with doing than with being. We seek ways "to be" by doing something. We sometimes confuse the two. Being and doing are two poles to our lives. They are flip sides of the same coin. They are not two separate coins.

We must remember that one calls us into the other and that we represent the melding of both, not one or the other. We must have practice and we must have stillness in order to be whole. Our wholeness as people spans the landscape of mystic encounters with God and sociopolitical endeavors with all mankind around us. We seek Divine Union and feed our hungering neighbors with one and the same person. Inside and outside, we are one.

If we practice a sitting exercise that reveals to us that we are currently and consciously fabricating a cell or a city about us, we are better apt to remember that the place we are living from is a creation of our own life and living. If we acknowledge we are building our reality we are more inclined to take responsibility for our reality.

We can learn to produce holiness unintentionally if we practice producing holiness intentionally first. We can add to our practices while sitting. We can imagine ourselves building a cell—a wooden or stone structure—around us while we sit. We imagine ourselves making a "Far Mosque."

We gather piles of stone or wood to build our cell. We name each stone or board. This one is "love." This one is "patience." This one is "forgiveness." This one is "visiting the sick." On and on we go, naming each piece of our structure to be.

We build, one stone or board at a time. When we are done, we imagine ourselves sitting back down, with Jesus at our side, sitting in our cell with us. We bring our attention back to Jesus when it wanders. If we lust for a mansion and not a cell, we add a new stone or piece of wood to our cell; this one is called "poverty" or "non-acquisitiveness." If we sense hatred while building, we add a new stone or piece of wood to our cell; this one is called "compassion." We build and we sit; intentionally.

By making the process of creation intentional we will also bring a clarifying awareness to what we are doing and hopefully utilize much more choice in the materials that we build with and from. We can make more progress.

～ ～ ～

We can expand these practices to include other scenes; other ways of imaging what we are creating here around us. But, as with all practices, the goal is for us to be able to be set free into laying aside the practice and just being in the presence of God. The practice is simply foreplay. Union comes when we are set free from images and practices all-together.

Find a place to pray. Sit there. Begin by simply imaging that your are in a cave. This is the cave of your own heart. Perhaps there might be a stream there, with a rock against which you could. Water is trickling over a small falls. The walls of the cave are covered with moss, and the ground covered with ferns. It is warm and inviting.

You can feel yourself there; simply sitting for the first few times you try this intention. Then perhaps you could imagine praying there. This is somehow your sacred prayer closet. Another time you could invite Jesus in to this space with you and you could offer prayers and praise to Him from within this space of your heart. You could confess to Him, adore Him, thank Him, and offer your supplications to Him.

You are creating this environment in the area that you have set aside for prayer. It will happen and grow in this place alone, at first. Eventually you will take this experience with you everywhere you go and will be able to enter into this encountering and wrestling while performing the routine tasks of daily life.

This practice will trickle in to the rest of your life. It will no longer simply be something that affects your prayers and ability to pray. Intentionality will implant itself in all you do—every habit and routine. Acts of kindness and mercy will be vilified by the notion of doing them with mindfulness.

No longer will you be acting compassionately in a childish way—to achieve gems and jewels for your heavenly crown. You will be acting compassionately because a deepening reflection reminds you that we are all in need and that there is no other way to live.

This form of renewal does not only work from the inside out; changing our outer habits because of our inward practice. It works from the outside in. The great practices of fasting, vigils, prostrations and the like all focus the outward life of the body onto a method that will help us to obtain inward peace and stillness.

Perhaps the most readily understandable method from many of the Fathers of the Church as well as the Talmud is the focusing of the eyes on the ground. This practice of averting the eyes is not simply a practice for our sitting, but for whenever we move from place to place. Averting one's eyes to the ground not only aids us by keeping our eyes from seeing things that may tempt us, but the very casting down of the vision illuminates our life with an interior humility. We see others as better than ourselves and are brought down low.

The Church developed prayers all through her history. These prayers were meant to take us into the terrain of God. Many of them were prayers of entering the Presence. These are call "prayers of entrance." They are image-full prayers that help us practice intentionally entering God's presence, just like the visualization practice listed above.

One such prayer comes from the Orthodox Tradition and is a part of every prayer service the Orthodox Christian offers. The prayer cries:

"O Heavenly King, Comforter, Spirit of Truth everywhere present and filling all things. Treasury of blessing and Giver of Life. Come and abide in us and cleanse us from every sin, and save our souls, O Good One."

We offer prayers like this to get us into a frame of mind to encounter and wrestle with God. They are the practice before the stillness. They get us ready for what should take place in prayer. They are never an end in themselves. They are meant to take us to the place of union and transformation in God. By using these prayers we are shaping the space around us and getting ready. We are developing a practice for sitting.

The desert ascetics used words like this to build communities in the wilderness. The landscape of their lives was marked with entrance prayers that enabled them to transcend simply existing as social beings among other social beings. Their lives were marked with practices as well—practices that also enabled them to transcend simply existing and become dwelling places of God. They lived as tabernacles of the Eternal.

Because they shifted the nature of life, the realities they saw were different from what they experienced in the cities of man. They saw angels and demons in the land.

As we begin to have an anchoring practice in our prayer spaces, we will notice a new reality emerging in our lives. It may not reveal angels and demons, but we will begin to notice things in a new light. We will recognize all people as potential tabernacles of God. We will sense a softer and more complex side to life. Simple didactic meaning will no longer be the sole aim of a religious life. We will hunger for ongoing and "growing" change in who we are.

For years, serving in Orthodox churches as a clergyman, I would pray these entrance prayers before the "Royal Gate" in the icon-screen, just this side of the altar. An emotion of humility would mount in me as I leaned toward the icon of Christ—bowing at the waist with hands upraised in the "orans" prayer posture.

Over and over, day in and day out these prayers would roll out of my mouth and enter into the air, creating an environment of humility and awe. My words taught my heart about reverence.

Eventually, that same ambience would fill the air in my home prayer-space as I offered the same prayers. Later, the woods would feel sacred as I offered the words in a forest. Now, wherever I am takes on the feel of that place when I offer these words of prayer. The repetition of the practice has built up a neural pathway that transcends and recreates the space around me. Praying these "prayers of entrance" has trained my heart in the craft of humility.

I believe this is what Saint Paul was getting at when he reminded us to be transformed by the renewing of the mind. We are to create new habits, holy habits that will transcend place and time and enable us to live in Christ—anywhere and anytime.

≈ ≈ ≈

"BECAUSE"

Because I made a space
in which to pray,
I can pray in any place
I take myself.

I must find
shelter in one space
to learn that sheltering
space is all around.
An image of one cave

becomes my sense of
cave anywhere –
Plato knew this.
Because I raised my
hands in one place,
I can raise them
in any place I go.
Because I sought God here.
I can go there and find Him,
just the same.

No matter how lofty we believe our inner discoveries are, the routine of cairn-space is the same. We set out with a practice or two, so we can enter into the space where no practice exists. We start doing, so we may find being. Once we have begun this process, we will find it is portable, traveling with us anywhere and anytime. Heaven and earth are joined and inhabit our heart. The heart is the eye of the storm.

In the words of the Hermetic Tradition found in the "Kybalion", the "Hermes Trismegistus", and teachings of Kashmir Shaivism, "As above, so below. As inside, so outside." The heart is the locus of all our work. The heart is the eye of the storm.

Chapter Eight

W E CAN HAVE THESE sessions of the heart often. The visualizations and prayer times we create in the heart—as spiritual practice—can lead into the deeper meditation and contemplation of silence and stillness as time goes by. They will also help us to shift the core of our identity into a holier place than they were before we began to pray.

There is really no limit to the creating of sacred moments in this space of the heart. The heart is deep; its depth has no end. The heart is the eye of the storm.

Simply sensing our awareness to be in the heart can change how we respond to things. The Institute of HeartMath has done studies on the efficacy of placing our attention in the heart region. They have actually developed tools to help people avert stress in their lives by placing their awareness in the heart and breathing.

These practices are not much different from the spiritual practices discussed in the Philokalia and the Hesychastic tradition (particularly the "somatopsychic techniques", see THE GUILD OF PASTORAL PSYCHOLOGY, GUILD LECTURE No. 95, ASCETICISM (Somatopsychic Techniques), By The Very Rev. ANTHONY BLOOM, M.D. (Paris)). The HeartMath studies have shown consistent entrainment of brainwaves to the rhythms in the heart while focusing the attention of the mind and the breath on the heart region. Going into the heart is not just a healthy spiritual practice, it is good for the overall health of our bodies as well.

The more we have these experiences, the more the sheaths of myelin are wrapped around the neural pathways of our heart-space. The more the sheaths of myelin are wrapped around our neural pathways of our heart-space, the easier it is for us to enter into this place.

Anthony DeMello wrote many books on the art of creative visualization in prayer. It is a practice we have discussed in earlier places in this book. The visualizations have the same entraining affect noted by HeartMath when we become aware of our visualizations happening within the heart, while connected to our breath. They bring the brain, the heart, and the breath into a unified field.

Perhaps the most daunting mysteries of the type of prayer DeMello teaches emerge from the practice of recreating scenes of the Gospels in which we imagine ourselves as the main characters. We engage in the unification of heart, mind and breath, but within the framework of conversion and transformation.

We read the stories of the Gospels, one at a time, and imagine ourselves there—right in the story. In one session we may image ourselves as the Prodigal Son. In another session, we may image ourselves as the Blind Bartimeaus.

We walk through the biblical narrative—in this practice—replacing the characters of the stories with our own selves. We sense how we would have responded in these parables. We ask ourselves if there is a better way to respond. We encounter and interact with God and His Son—a wrestling to be sure. All of this may occur in this same cave of the heart.

The practice has an immense impact on our lives as we begin to see the Gospels as guidebooks to relationship and not simply historical data from the days of the Savior. The Gospels are real, alive, and contain the momentum of spirit that can change our lives. They are not merely didactic material for sermons and workshops. The Gospels are initiation tools for the journey of becoming divinized by the Spirit of God.

We must simply choose to interact with them as such. When we do interact with them, we are transformed into the very characters we read about. We are changing our neural pathways. We entrain our hearts and minds and breath into the Gospel story.

There is a practice I crafted out of a Tibetan meditation (similar in nature to DeMello's visualizations) known as the Jewel Tree. I have adapted it to my Christian vision of life. It is a tool for receiving from Jesus, the very nature of who He is. It is very centering. It connects us deeply with Jesus.

Bob Thurman has written about this Tibetan meditation practice in his book, "The Jewel Tree of Tibet: The Enlightenment Engine of Tibetan Buddhism." The practice of this particular Tibetan meditation falls into the category of mentor deity yoga or mentor deity meditation. That is, meditation on God/Mentor, in such a way as to build a connective bridge from God/Mentor to the disciple/practitioner. It is a visualization of the transmission energies from God/Mentor to disciple/practitioner. It is like receiving the baptism of the Holy Spirit; the transmission that Jesus offers us in our path of "theosis."

As a Jesus-believer, I replaced the central image of the Buddha/Mentor with Jesus. Thurman himself makes the same recommendation. I also shifted some things around to suit my current meditation and prayer practice. Therefore, if you are familiar with the text, you will notice my practice to be a slight deviation of the meditation.

We imagine Jesus as our God/Mentor. He is the One who gifts us with the skill and ability to do the things in life we hope to do—the things we feel called to accomplish. In our practice (described in a minute) we take from Jesus the gifts He has to bestow. We place them inside our heart. We then offer back to Jesus the gifts we have to share.

God, our mentor, (in this meditation) gives us what we need to become fashioned more and more in His image and likeness. We take these gifs from God, place them in our heart, and offer up our hearts and lives as a living sacrifice to Him in return.

This giving and taking helps us recognize our connection to Him, our mentor deity. It enables us to become transformed by a relationship of giving and taking with Jesus. We will visualize—in the practice to come—placing Jesus and or the gifts of Jesus into our heart. This is how we are transformed. This is how we are made holy. This is how we participate in the divine nature.

The Fathers of the Church clearly taught (and it is sadly lost in today's church) the notion of "theosis." This is the process of becoming divinized by God. It is the process of our salvation over time. We become holy, sanctified, and divinized. We are to become BY GRACE, what Christ is BY NATURE. That is, we are to become divine; we enter into the Divine Milieu and are transformed.

Most modern churchmen cringe at this idea and holler out, "New Age." The truth is, this is "Early Church" and was, in their understanding, the whole reason God came down to us in the first place. God seeks to bring us back to our divine status as sons and daughters of the Most High. Saint Athanasios (my patron), along with other Church Fathers taught, "God became man, that men might become God (divine).

As a church of modernity, we have forgotten many of the rituals and routines that remind us of the persons we truly are—the persons we have forgotten. There is no wonder that modern church-goers find a discussion of theosis and divinization to be out of place.

We have stricken the practices of theosis out of the contemporary spiritual canon. We have removed the sacraments—agents of theosis—from the lives of church-folk and replaced them with programs to grow our church's numerical presence in the community.

Bringing God into our lives transforms us. It makes us partakers of the Divine Nature. We have chosen to cheapen the Divine Nature instead of elevating our human nature. We have "dumbed-down" Divinity rather than "celestializing" humanity.

We imagine ourselves seated in a comfortable position. Our palms are lying open in our lap, one on top of the other. In front of us, we imagine Jesus. He is also seated in a similar position and His hands are in His lap, as well.

We imagine that the LORD is seated on a small island, surrounded by an ocean or great lake. Behind Him is a tall tree of blessing and mirth. The tree is filled with dazzling jewels We imagine the LORD is iridescent blue. He radiates great warmth and connection from every pore of His body. His eyes fixed on our eyes. Everything that radiates from Him, radiates into us. We receive from Him all that He exudes. We imagine Him also in our heart.

From our seated place we bow before Him. Touching our forehead to the ground in humility and obeisance, we prostrate before Him. We sit up and gaze on the beauty of the LORD.

We imagine Jesus reaching into the tree and choosing a jewel of splendid color—perhaps gold. He tells us, "This is my love" and He hands it to us. He asks us to place it in our heart. We do. We feel its warmth.

He then reaches into the tree and selects a green jewel. He tells us, "This is my peace." Again, He hands it to us and we place it in our heart, feeling its warmth. He does this again and again. He hands us grace, mercy, understanding, wisdom, joy, patience, kindness, gentleness, self-control, and adoration. We place them all in our heart and we feel the presence of these dazzling and brilliant gifts. The gifts of the Master radiate into our every pore and make us like Him. We thank Him.

We then imagine that He is seated in our heart. The one before us is also within us. As He sits there—in our heart—we imagine that He is surrounded by all of the gifts He has just given us. We imagine ourselves reaching into our chest and removing our heart. Holding it up to the LORD in front of us, we tell Him, "This heart is yours." We replace our heart into our chest and bow, again, before Him.

This exercise is not very different from some of the ones that have come down to us through the history of the Church. In particular, I am thinking of some of the Sacred Heart of Jesus meditations and visualizations.

There is a corollary meditation that is similar. In this visualization, we reach into our heart and take out gifts to offer Jesus. The gifts are the same, they are the jewels of the spiritual life: grace, mercy, understanding, wisdom, joy, patience, kindness, gentleness, self-control, and adoration. This time, we offer them to Christ to bless and give back to us. We go through the imaginings of Him blessing each jewel and giving it back to us at the end. We place them back into our heart. We thank Him.

What is essential in this visualization practice is the sense of give and take to and from the mentor deity and the practitioner. Whether we begin the practice by offering to Jesus, or we begin the practice by Jesus offering to us it does not matter. What is important is the connection to Jesus. What is also important is the back and forth nature of the giving and receiving. We give and we receive; Jesus gives and Jesus receives. We are giving ourselves and receiving Jesus. Jesus is giving Himself and receiving us.

This practice, although inspired by the Tibetan Jewel Tree, is a glom of practices I have utilized in visualization technique from the East and from the West. The aim is that we see ourselves creating not only a space, but an attitude from things that we ourselves have within us—things we have received from God. It elevates our lives and gives us ennobling qualities to strive for and to build with—all under the watchful eye and blessing of Jesus.

I love the image of Jesus as blue. Although it has implications from Eastern practice outside of the Church, there are many references within the Eastern Christian teachings of finding a blue pearl or blue light within—particularly among the "Pearlers" (Syrian Christian mystics of the 6th and 7th centuries). The "blue man" also appears in the mystic treatises and illuminations of Abbess Hildegard of Bingen from the Western Medieval Christian Church. The tradition of Hesychasm in Orthodoxy acknowledges these same images of "sapphire blue" light in prayer. It is a calming and enriching color that spans many traditions and many centuries of interior work.

Last summer, my sons and I were taking a daily run. It was a way of spending time together amid the busy schedule of life at a camp and retreat center. At the end of the run we would practice a simple workout routine from a karate school in the United States. Once the routine was finished, we would sit in meditation for a while. One of the practices that we would often use in this meditation time was that of the Jewel Tree.

I would verbally walk them through one of the exercises described above. It gave us a point of departure toward sharing an interior life together. It was very powerful for us. It opened us to a deeper connection with Jesus and each other.

This is not the only practice the heart can hold. The heart is deep; its depths have no end. As with all practices of prayer-space, they are to lead us to a place of silence and stillness before God.

It should not take much imagination to see the Jewel Tree visualization as an extension of what happens as we sit in stillness anyway. We have mentioned that in our approaching stillness (after our spiritual practice) we often see things arise—things that come up from inside us and make their way out—to the surface of consciousness.

In the Jewel Tree meditation we are simply choosing the things that arise from within. We could just as easily do the meditation and offer Jesus the impatience, lust, greed, and other spontaneous arisings that seek to distract us from stillness.

We could imagine Him blessing the arisings and converting them to jewels (lust turned to golden appreciation; greed turned to an emerald openness, etc.) that we place back in our heart. One form is planned and the other form is spontaneous. This is just like the nature of either directive or non-directive approaches in therapy. Both take us into the heart. The heart is the eye of the storm.

The "Pearlers", as Brian E. Colless calls the Syrian Christian mystics in his book "the Wisdom of the Pearlers", spoke often of the image of the pearl in the spiritual life. The Syriac manuscript of the "Acts of Thomas" has a hymn embedded in it entitled "The Song of the Pearl" also known as the "Hymn of the Soul." The hymn relates a story of a son's arduous journey to find a pearl hidden in the depths of the sea.

The son is sent on his journey by his father and mother (a king and queen). While on the journey, he forgets his mission. He is reminded to take up his quest to find the pearl in a letter he receives from his father.

The imagery is ripe for spiritual interpretation. As with other Gnostic hero journeys, there is a palpable feel to the story that reminds us we are all here on this earth to recover something for our Father. From this story, Colless weaves a tale of connectivity by translating the writings of the Syrian Fathers and allowing us to read over and over again the imagery they use for the kingdom of God—imagery wrapped around the notion of diving and discovering the elusive pearl within.

The significance of the pearl might be lost on some who have not entered into the meditative space of the heart. But, for those who have, they will recognize the visions of light that one discovers after the arisings of mental and emotional imagery have ceased.

Once we have found episodes of stillness and silence within, a very clear image of interior light appears. The light is often golden and or iridescent blue. The lights may appear individually or in close proximity to one another. They may actually emanate from one another. The Syraic Fathers called this the light of the sun and the sapphire light. It is shaped like a pearl. It often pulsates or radiates.

The images of the inner pearl are validated over and over again in the translations of the Pearlers texts. The light within is a joyous reward for discovering stillness in prayer.

Most of the ascetic athletes "saw" the light as the light of the soul in the body. They believed that prolonged exposure to this inner light of the soul would fall away and the believer would eventual see the "Uncreated Light" of the Energies of God that dwell in all creation. Purification produces enlightenment: the vision of the light of the soul and God's Uncreated Energies.

Exposed to this light within over and over again, it is taught that the believer will eventually enter complete stillness and silence where there is no vision of anything. There is only absorption in the Divine.

Although images and impressions of demons are present at the outset of the inner journey, and images and impressions of light are present at the second stage of the inner journey, abolition of images and impressions marks the third stage of the journey. In this final phase of prayer, there is only Light—formless and all encompassing Light. This Light is often spoken of as pure blackness. We move from form to the formless.

Joseph the Visionary and John the Venerable remind us, as do the other Syrian Fathers, that when we approach this stage of prayer, we become consumed by it. As the merchant who found a pearl buried in a field and sold all he had to buy the field, we will lay aside all earthly cares to "purchase" and enter the formless presence of the Light.

It is clear in the texts that we can only pass through this process one step at a time. The hard work of spiritual practice cannot be replaced. We must first sit and deal with all that arises so we can move beyond the arisings into the luminous field of God's presence beneath the arisings.

Some have classified the journey as moving from the mind into the heart into the soul and finally into spirit/Spirit. The mind has thought forms that we must process: memories, thoughts, and ideas. The heart has emotional forms that we must process: emotions, feelings, and impressions. The soul has drives that we must process: desires, longings, and hopes. Passing through all of these we are set free to experience the light of the spirit/Spirit and its source—the Uncreated Energies of God. The practices enable us to deal with all that arises in these areas and ultimately achieve a stillness and silence that is truly rest.

Hildegard of Bingen, born in the twelfth century, had had visions of God since the age of three. She began writing and then sketching her visions. The corpus of her work is a bold statement of contemplative freedom and joy. Her visions were not only filled with Divine images and images of light, but also of the strains of music and the healing power of herbs. She went on to produce great pieces of music and tomes of information on gardens and medicine in addition to her works on the inner journey.

One of the recurring images that appears in her drawings is clearly of the pearl of the Pearlers. She drew scintillating orbs of light, most often blue and gold. She also drew images of a "sapphire man", wrapped in mandalas of light. Seeing her works and having a basic knowledge of meditation and the writings of the interior mystics, one cannot believe this is a coincidence.

There is something about the inner journey that people have experienced that transcends time and locale. There is a luminous baseline to the experiences of mystics.

We could consider the imagery Christian if it were not for the fact that tomes of literature from Shaivism (Shiva devotees) did not also report similar findings. The blue pearl and the blue man are the object of meditation over and over again in Hindu writings.

This sapphire light and sapphire man, as well as the golden light seem to appear as a calming manifestation of the Divine presence. Reports of them have been a harbinger of peace and fondness. They do not reveal horror or fear. They seem to reveal that some form of purification has begun and that the experience of enlightenment is unfolding in the individual.

Eventually, when we are able to pass through all of the chatter of the mind and heart, we will find a field within. When we find the field, we will discover that it holds a pearl of great price. We will be willing to sell everything we posses to buy that field and obtain the pearl. The more we have these experiences, the more the sheaths of myelin are wrapped around the neural pathways of heart-space.

Chapter Nine

"CRICKET SPACE"

There is a space
on the other side
of the lake;

a space where
a cricket can
crawl
between
the rock and the
moss that is leaning
up
against
the tree.

A space
just
small enough
to hide
from the wind
and the rain that
drives itself
against
the calm.

I shall find

THAT space.

There
I shall
hunker down
and listen
for the sound of
the growing roots

and the seeping
rain

and the
sound
of brittle leaves
blowing over
the rocks.

The branches
there
are
tossed about
on the
ground,
brittle peelings
of bark
making other spaces
for the crickets
to shelter nicely
when wind and rain
are not driving.

It is quiet there,
in these hiding places.
And calm;

did I say calm?

~ ~ ~

This is not the only way to approach the interior prayer-space. These methods utilize the imagination to help create a space and an environment from within which prayer can occur. A place that can hold union, too. According to the teachings of the Fathers of interior prayer, this type of prayer is elementary.

The fullest form of prayer uses no words, no thoughts, no feelings, and no images. The fullest and deepest place of prayer is stillness within the heart. Most of these teachings come from Evagrios.

This territory—stillness—is seldom visited in the life of modern people. Nevertheless, many tales are being told; and many wanderers are seeking to find this path and this practice today. The young want to rise up out of the aridity that has become a surrounding environment for the modern Church.

The new Church is clambering to experience and practice the presence of God. After all, this is what it means to be "Church" in the first place. Church is a people becoming a tabernacle for the Divine One.

Seeing the art of crafting space as something we are always doing, and taking an active role in crafting intentionally holy lives and space is only the beginning of the interior life. It is only the first cairn-space we create. As time goes on, as practice richens and deepens, a stillness is built. We are able to craft a vortex of peace, a black hole of holiness.

There was an Eastern Orthodox saint from Russia named Saint Seraphim of Sarov. His life was an ongoing ritual of intentional obedience and stillness. At one point in his life, he radiated the inner light of Christ to such an extent that a man speaking with him had to cover his eyes. The process of divinization was so immense in him that the "Light of Tabor" escaped his every pore.

Saint Seraphim of Sarov is noted for a humility of Christ-like-ness that simply crawled out of his being—body and soul. He is most noted for saying, "Seek inner-peace, and thousands will be saved around you."

This master of the inner way was plain in his teaching. If you want to have the greatest impact for Christ that you can have, then, tidy up your inner life, find stillness with Jesus inside, and it will change the world around you. He taught that the acquisition of God (through the Holy Spirit) was the goal of the Christian life. We acquire the Holy Spirit in the stillness of the heart.

One element of this holy stillness is also called "apatheia" by the Fathers. It is detachment. It is a state of desireless desire. The flight to the desert—to cairn-spaces—is always a flight from chaos into apatheia. The monks and nuns of the desert sought to abandon the busy-ness of life in the Empire to find peace; to find a calm away from the turmoil. All of our seeking of prayer-space is an attempt to remove ourselves from flurry of activity and enter into the rest of God; enter into the Sabbath of life. We move from feverish clutching to non-acquisition.

Just like the "cricket-space" in the poem, there are a thousand and one images of small retreating places that we find all around us. We see a cave in the woods, or a quiet meadow by a lake; we notice an isolated stand of tall pines or a knob that overlooks a vista and our heart longs to be there. Our soul cries out to enter this place. We dream of getting away. We long for rest and solitude.

This is the yearning of our lives for stillness. We seek places in which we can disconnect and recharge. Sleep itself becomes a Sabbath oasis in which we can plug into some greater energy; the energy of inertia. There is a power in stillness. It is the power that emanated from Saint Seraphim as God's whole Fire and Light.

O Most Holy Trinity, have mercy on us!
Lord, wash away our sins!
Master, pardon our transgressions!
Holy One, visit and heal our infirmities for Thy name's sake.

Glory to the Father, and to the Son, and to the Holy Spirit, now and ever and unto ages of ages. Amen.

Lord, have mercy! (3 times)
Holy God, Holy Mighty, Holy Immortal have mercy on us.
Holy God, Holy Mighty, Holy Immortal have mercy on us.
Holy God, Holy Mighty, Holy Immortal have mercy on us.
Amen.
—PRAYER TO THE MOST HOLY TRINITY, THE ORTHODOX PRAYERBOOK

≈ ≈ ≈

A central theme in spiritual growth is coming to terms with our aloneness. We all feel alone at some point in our lives—sometimes more often than not. One of the things that modern worship averts us from is feeling alone. So many individuals and groups cannot even begin to think about approaching aloneness because they are so paralyzed by issues and images of abandonment.

We know that aloneness enters into the nature of being. God is community—Father, Son, and Holy Spirit—and calls us into community when He says, "It is not good that man is alone." God creates community for us. God gives this community a garden—sacred space. Somewhere in our lives, then, we must come to grips with aloneness, community, and the sacred space within which they dwell. These are "central themes."

Being alone with the Alone is the goal of a life of stillness and silence. We hope that we may gain a sense that we are with God—nothing else but God. We are trying to remember God and nothing else. When we do, the Alone removes our aloneness by His presence.

Our practices help us to arrive at this place. Our images and thoughts may be used to attain access. Our watchfulness may prepare us for His presence. It seems that our hungering for cricket-spaces and little hide-aways is a therapeutic yearning to deal with the concepts of isolation and loneliness.

Once we are in sacred-space, everything must drop away so we may simply be with God. We must lose the practices that we hold onto in order to maintain our balance. The height of the spiritual life is being with God—with no props.

But, we need the props to get us there safely. They show us the way.

This union is the most transformative action of inaction available to the believer. It changes who we are in every other moment of our lives. When we are alone with the Alone, we are no longer alone—nor is He.

Many faiths have a concept that speaks to the elusiveness of God. God hides from us. He is concealed behind all that He chooses. We must find Him.

Our journey of sacred-space, cairn-space, and prayer-space is all about the process of finding the practices that help us uncover the identity of the Concealed One in the stillness of the heart; help us approach the Hidden One. When we have uncovered the Identity, we are at our prize. When we have found the Hidden One, He is no longer hidden. The heart is the eye of the storm.

There is a riddle hidden in this quest. The riddle is that our own identity is hidden to us. The fullness of spiritual therapy is when we realize that we are not only searching for the Hidden Self, but the hidden self. There is some neural pathway between the individual soul and the Divine Soul. There is a link between the ego, and the Self: between the I and the I AM.

The concept of dissolving the ego shows up so many times in spiritual traditions precisely because we know there is a connection, we sense there is a dependency. In our brashness we have believed we must obliterate the one to partake of the Other. In fact, what cairn-space teaches us is that we must pass through the ego to enter into God. We must wrestle with the individual self to partake of Divine union. The ego is dissolved only when it is in union with the Great Self. It becomes hidden in the Ultimate Reality.

≈ ≈ ≈

O Lord and Master of my life,
Grant not unto me a spirit of idleness,
of discouragement,
of lust for power,
and of vain speaking.
(low prostration to the floor)
But bestow upon me, Thy servant,
the spirit of chastity,
of meekness,
of patience,
and of love.
(low prostration to the floor)
Yea, O Lord and King,
grant that I may perceive
my own transgressions,
and judge not my brother,
for blessed art Thou
unto ages of ages.
Amen.
(low prostration to the floor)
—THE PRAYER OF SAINT EPHRAIM, THE ORTHODOX PRAYERBOOK

Chapter Ten

"THE BONES OF CALLIXTUS"

There are bones in there,
that is why they came.
To offer bread,
to offer wine–
they came to the place
that housed the kingdom,
the place of the
bones of the Church.
A bone is in the
wood of the altar.
Panteleimon,
I believe.
In the center of the
Mensa, it sits and waits.
He sits and waits.
He awaits the coming
of the One who left,
he awaits the coming
of the children
of Bread and Wine.
In defiance
the children of Luther
told the world
they did not need bones
to give testimony to
the Presence of the One.
They lost their
anchor of bones

to the full
weight of glory
on that day.
They exchanged meeting
God in tandem
with solitary upheaval.
Where there are
no bones to make space
holy
there are no saints calling
us beyond our singular
experience to meet
the One with
the train of time.
There is no flesh
that is changed
by cradling God.
The Virgin has
lost her place,
and so have all
of us
if the bones mean nothing.
We have moved
away from our
connection to the bones
of the invisible Church.
What happens
when the Bread and the Wine
are no longer God?
What happens when we say
we do not need matter
to experience the Divine?
We find another form.
Perhaps a golden calf.
We will always find matter
a ladder to the
meeting. We
should not be fooled

into thinking we
can do it any other way.
When we push away the
sacredness of space
we ultimately say
redemption cannot
save our bones,
Bread and Wine cannot
transfigure us.
God does not dwell
in our flesh.
I long for
the house of bones
that are my comrades
in the struggle.
I hunger for a space that
is holy. Where is that
place? Where is
the flesh
that is a platform
for the Divine One?

~ ~ ~

The discussion about place is a discussion about the relevance of matter in our lives. When we talk about having sacred-spaces that serve as launching off places for the spiritual journey, we are talking about sacramental lives. Lives in which this can represent that. Matter can house meaning that is beyond its own confines. Place can mean dimension, depth, pathway.

A few key discussions in the early Church development of dogma and kerygma became "tells" of whether or not you were in the proper theological camp. They were sort of "secret handshakes" if you will. These "critical issues" let people know whether your understanding of the incarnation was the same as theirs; or if you had subtle differences in belief and understanding. These "critical issues" let people know where you were in your belief about who Jesus was.

Two of these critical issues were the "relics of the saints" and the "Theotokos" (God-Bearer). Knowing what you believed about the saints and the Virgin Mary could weed out whether you were orthodox or heretical in your thinking. It was a question of whether or not you really believed that matter could contain the Divine.

If you believed that matter could fully contain the Divine then you would have had a highly developed view of the saints and the Virgin Mary. Ultimately, this meant that you had a sophisticated enough (one with depth and complexity) view of Jesus and the incarnation.

Did your view sustain the belief that He was 100% God and 100% man; two natures in one person? Add to these "critical issues" the teachings on the Eucharist, theosis, and the Essence/Energies and you have a full portfolio of options for defining the presence of the Divine among the creation and figuring out just exactly where you landed on beliefs about how that actually was possible. You could divine a persons stand on all of the issues listed above, simply by knowing their connection to the saints and the Virgin Mary.

How far does your understanding of sacred-space really go?

In the early Church, the celebration of the Eucharist happened in homes, in catacombs, and on the graves of the saints. The faithful gathered at the tombs to remember the brothers and sisters who had died. They gathered and broke the bread and drank the wine. They gathered and prayed.

In the homes, there were often frescoes on the walls depicting Christ, the saints, and the Old Testament pre-figurations of Christ. The early believers shared the sacraments there amid the memory of those who had gone on before them.

Dura-Europos, c. AD 230 in what is present day Iraq, is the earliest extant house-church that we know of. There is no record of the bones of the saints being present at the services of Dura-Europos, simply the depiction of holy figures on the walls. It was important to gather together and to do so in the presence of all time. We know there was a baptistery there, a Eucharistic mensa, and a store-room for food for the poor. There may also have been a study there.

The Church gave memory to the saints and to the One who asked to be remembered at every gathering—the One who appeared to them in the breaking of the bread. Sacred space was reserved for remembering God and the people of God, and celebrating the Holy Mystery that brings the two together. Sacred space has always been about encounter and wrestling.

Having the relics of the saints present was a homecoming; it was also a reminder that God dwelt in matter. Those who had died and had gone to eternal rest to pray for the Church of Christ, were incorporated into services by the presence of their bones. God was present, not just in some ethereal way, but concretely in that He had dwelt in these bones—somehow. It added depth to the hope.

The faithful told stories of the lives of the saints, of their deaths, of their teachings. People took courage during the persecutions by sharing the lives of the saints, and keeping them around in memory through their relics. But, they were also a piece of physical matter that was said to have housed the Divine. God lived in the saints, so at some level their flesh was different—somehow transformed. Somehow we were, too.

When celebrating at the graveside or in the catacombs fell out of use, (mostly after the adoption of Christianity as the Imperial Religion under Constantine) the cult of relics rose in practice. The saints became portable. You did not any longer go to them; you brought them to you.

Eventually, this became the norm for establishing a Church building; relics were placed in the altar at the consecration of the building. This gave testimony to the fullness of the Church—both the visible and invisible people of God. It reminded people where they came from. Sacred space was set by the bones of the community. Sacred time was announced in the presence of sacred space. Holiness was something that affected time, space, and individuals. Holiness was important. Just as God in the saints changed them, the presence of the saints could change us.

Adhering to this tradition was a way of upholding the memory of the complete body of Christ and the fullness of the incarnation. Without the saints, we are simply not the fullness we were meant to be. We lose our bearings when we do not remember from whom we have been birthed. It is a cairn-less land when we have no bones; no history, no saints and martyrs. Flesh no longer houses the Divine.

Later, in Church history, believers gave up the notion of solidifying the kingdom with the bone testimonies of the saints. They felt it unnecessary. They could be the Church without bones. Abuses in the Church (selling bones and making them a focus of worship and salvation) helped the believers decide to do away with relics all together.

Although it is true that our individual faith does not require the saints be made known to us in our worship for worship to happen, we surely are the less for not including the full Bride of Christ from all ages into our prayers and adoration.

We have moved away from developing and teaching—as well as understanding—a context for worship. It also says a whole lot about whether we truly believe the Divine presence does in fact dwell in flesh and matter.

With all of the "trappings" and "kerygma" removed from our worship, we are left as a stark and naked Church standing on its own belief at that moment in time. The richness of faith and worship is lost when we execute the witness of history from our memories.

Those who fail to remember the past are surely condemned to repeat it (George Santanyana). Should we really get rid of our past? Without these moorings we have no place to begin our worship. We are left having to ask ourselves, "What is it we want to do today?" When we gather as Church we get to make up our own list of priorities. This says that we believe there is nothing that has been handed down to us that we think is necessary. We have disavowed ourselves from the meaning that comes with being an historic body. We separate ourselves from the record of "God with man abiding."

I notice with the removal of these pieces of our past from our worship places, (including the total denuding of places of worship) that we have also disavowed any connection to the teachings and beliefs of the Church from the past. This is dangerous. Our belief only came down to us because of the millions of believers who professed and attested to it through the ages. The believers from Apostolic times until now have value and meaning in the life of the Church today. Where are they? The Church is a process and an event. The Church is everything the people of God have gathered through time, and what we have to offer. It is not just about us, right here, and right now. If it was, the crucifixion would be meaningless.

Many Churches disavow the teachings of the Fathers of the Church and teach scripture alone is all that is needed for the life and health of the Church today. These same contemporary believers have no knowledge that the very Fathers they deride have been the selectors of the canon itself.

The Fathers were used by God to cull out the wheat and the tares of all the sacred texts that were being passed back and forth in the Christian world at the time. The Fathers, in the first Church council at Nicea—AD 325—rejected dozens of "scriptures" as non-canonical. Without the Fathers, there would be no Bible as we know it.

Many Churches have thrown out the creeds. These believers say that they do not need formulas for their belief. The creeds give shape to our belief. The creeds give us teachings like "and in the Son of God, Light from Light, True God from True God, begotten not made . . . "

How does one who grows up without the creeds really know the boundaries of who Jesus is? Have we allowed ourselves to believe that whatever we believe or say about Jesus is truth? The words of our theological parameters were developed into creeds to help us stay within the bounds of acceptable truth.

I only mention these facts tangential to our concerns. Some people will say—in keeping with pieces of the above logic—we do not need to set aside chapels, cells, prayer corners, cairns, and places for prayer. Prayer, in their estimation can and should happen anywhere. Although this is true—prayer can be offered anywhere—I would challenge us to look at the depth and nature of prayer that develops in these barren environs.

When we remove the structures of liturgy, Church teachings throughout the ages, and other traditional and historic connections to the development of the Spirit with us, we remove a balanced focus. When we begin to dismantle the phenomenology of faith and practice, then we begin to cheapen and devalue complex meaning. This can only lead to an emptiness that is on the verge of nihilism.

I have often left contemporary services of worship wondering what, if anything, just happened. The whole thing seemed to have been just about "us." There was no sense of God. Removing a connection to the Church throughout the ages certainly has left us more time to dumb-down the Gospels, have more meetings, more capital campaigns, and to dream up new ways use sound systems and PowerPoint presentations.

I am not suggesting that all Churches everywhere come up with some unified structure of faith and worship. When that was in place in history, it only fragmented itself into what we have today. What I am pointing at is that each body of faithful believers should spend some time with the questions:

What is sacred space?

What has the Church of the past left for us to help us?

How does worship reflect our belief?

How can we stay connected to the witness of the saints?

Where do liturgies, prayers, and creeds from Church history fit into our current faith and worship?

How do we create holy, sacred space?

Are we really meeting about the things that matter in eternity?

Do we really need to build more buildings?

Are we worshipping or entertaining?

What about establishing house Churches?

What is prayer?

How does our sense of Incarnation trickle down into other beliefs?

What do we believe about God abiding in creation?

What does it mean that the Virgin Mary bore God?

It is clear that every Church starts with its own set of presuppositions when it comes to its structure of faith and worship. Who is bringing these presuppositions out, dusting them off, and making them alive in congregations today? Have we slipped back into having abhorrent convocations and new moon celebrations? Isaiah told us these were displeasing to God (Isaiah i, 13).

In a day and age when denominationalism is being dismantled, we are looking at future generations of Churches that may have no spiritual oversight of any kind. Can this be good?

Our establishment of cairn-spaces and places of prayer give us the heart to begin to help the Church address some of these lost concerns. When we find the cell within, the prayer closet Jesus reminds us of, we hunger to see other people find this sacred space. We begin to long to see our corporate worship become sign and symbol of meeting God—within and without. How do our Churches reflect this yearning?

Prayer-space is not only vital for individuals. It is vital for the whole body of Christ's Church—throughout time. How will we go about addressing the issues of holiness, sacred-space, and "tabernacling" God in the modern Church?

If you have ever smelled the sweet aroma of the bones of a "myrrh-gushing" saint, or been in the presence of a miracle working relic or icon, you will know that sacred space does exist around people and objects. Something transfigures human flesh and material objects into containers of grace and power.

There is something amazing about certain places, certain things, and certain people. God has touched them. In many traditions it is believed that entering into the silent stillness of God, into union with the Holy, is what supercharges people with grace and power. The Holy Spirit is acquired more and more with each visit. Moses' face because of being in God's presence, Saint Seraphim shone because of being in God's presence.

This is what is accounted for in theologies of sanctification. Sanctification is the process of becoming sacred-space. It is a process and not an event. We grow into our divinity in Christ. We soak Him up, more and more over time (when we are attentive). We become divinized by Christ.

"HOUSE OF BONES"

I like
that they have
an ossuary
on the grounds;
a place to save their dead.
Some things should
not be thrown away.
They keep them all
neatly arranged –
the bones in boxes
and the skulls in rows.
names are carefully
scribbled on the skulls
with dates of birth and death

as best they know,
as best as they
keep time in these monasteries
of prayer and seclusion with the ONE.
I miss the bones
of the monks.
I see nothing that reminds me
I am next, I will die.
I just see pretty buildings
of comfort and ease;
a Church developed past its
own issues of death and grace,
a Church that hides
its skeletons
who knows where.
Who will remind
us that our
bones can hold God?
How shall we learn?

All of the monasteries we visited on the isle of Tinos, Greece had charnel houses—bone houses. These ossuaries were constructed to hold the bones of the departed. They were sort of a holding place for the saints until the resurrection of the dead.

If one of the brothers or sisters was extremely holy, their bodies may not have decayed in the temporary marble vaults used to decompose the flesh and prepare the bones for storage. The ones who did not decay often produced "the aroma of sanctity." There bones had an otherworldly smell; richer and deeper than the smell of roses.

Miracles were often performed in the presence of these holy ones— these bones. Saint Nektarios was like this. He is a modern Orthodox saint.

Who are the saints of this day? How does God inhabit them? Where are the miracles of healing and transformation? In removing cairn-space from our lives, have we removed the possibility of producing saints? The desert was filled with saints. The desert housed men and women who housed God.

Chapter Eleven

AT SOME POINT IN the discussion, we must ask ourselves what we feed on to become capable of creating an interior space of grandeur and awe, a heart of humility and grace. A place to tabernacle God. How will we sustain creating a sacred space in and around us? It requires a special diet.

The answer that comes from the Fathers is to make sacred space in the presence of others who seek to do the same. We need to create a community of support.

Yes, there were some Fathers that were able to go it alone. There were some that would rise above to become the images that others yearned after—sought to become. But for the most part, they are not who we are.

Even the isolates of the desert spent some time with other people, even if it was to give away their prized wisdom. We should seek a small community of seekers to be a part of; or at least pair ourselves up with one "spiritual friend" who can listen to our discoveries from prayer-space. We need people we can practice with; people who understand the stillness.

When we talk to others about our prayer-space, we are also allow-ing ourselves to hear what it is we are saying. We are enabled to hear the process of our own journey when we speak it to others. There must be a community we gain nourishment from, a body of seekers where we can gain guidance and relief.

This is really why we gather as Church. We gather to worship the Holy One. We gather to sit in His presence and become His Image and Likeness—His tabernacle. We come together to provide support for the journey. Much of what we do in our modern gathering as believers is work on ways to support the machine and programs of the machine, not encourage sanctification. How will we change this? Can we rewrite theosis into the DNA of the Church code?

Collectively we become the neural space in which God lives and moves and has His being. In this sense, we are the mind of God. Each of us a neural pathway of communicating axons and dendrites: information flowing through the field of the Divine.

The desert Christian communities developed the tradition of asking the Fathers for a "word." They would ask for a teaching from the masters of the interior life. "Give us a word, Father", was a common desert request and greeting.

This practice of asking for a "word" is needed today. It is another part of our diet. If you were to ask your pastor to give you a "word", what would they say? What would you say if you were asked for a "word"? Do you have anything to offer?

When we practice the interior life we have a lot to offer. We also have a lot we need to receive. Placing ourselves in situations where we can give and receive a "word", a teaching is important.

Sometimes the "word" the Fathers gave was a visual teaching, too. One of my favorite patristic "koans" from the desert saints is from Abba Moses. It comes from the Apophthegmata Patrum.

A brother from Scetis had committed a fault. A council was convened to judge the brother and assign a penance. Abba Moses was invited to the council, but refused to go. One of the Fathers sent a messenger to get Abba Moses to attend. The messenger begged Moses to attend, claiming that they were all waiting for him. Abba Moses got up, took a leaking jug and filled it with water and headed on his way to the council. When the elders ran out to greet him, someone asked, "Father, what is this?" Abba Moses replied, "My sins run out behind me all day long and I do not see them, and yet you expect me to judge this brother." They instantly understood and forgave the brother his sin.

Who will give us a word today?

The Benedictine monastic communities have developed the "Chapter of Faults." It is spurred on in practice by the 46th chapter of the Rule of Saint Benedict. Brothers are encouraged to gather the community and the abbot and confess any faults they have committed. The penance is to be lighter if they confess openly, rather than waiting until someone else points out their error.

It was a way of clearing the conscience and obtaining forgiveness in a community where everything done affected the whole group. It was a path toward healing.

Families are no different. Churches are no different. The actions of each member of any community impact the lives of all of the others. How have we allowed for reparation of our sins within our communities? Have we made repentance something that is solely a personal affair? Are we limiting the grace and nurturance that can be developed in community by the mutual bearing of one another's sins? Have we stifled the work of the Holy Spirit and radically altered the nature of community and grace?

We need to feed ourselves a diet of humble contrition, repentance, and forgiveness. These things nourish us and our communities.

For all intents and purposes, it feels as if the Church has lost its roots. It feels as if inner practices and small communities of growth and accountability are all but absent from the shape of the modern Church.

Reestablishing each would bring a modicum of balance back into the life of what appears to be an ailing dinosaur. This new monasticism would deepen the heart of the Church. It would provide space for us to meet God and experience the transformation of becoming BY GRACE, what Christ is BY NATURE. Without the creation of sacred-space—cairn-space—we stand to lose the very soul of what it means to be Church: a Divine encounter with Jesus that opens us to purification, enlightenment, and union with God.

If we build the space into our own lives, we will begin to hunger for it in our communities. If we build it into our communities, we will become a city on a hill. All of the world will want what we have; a space where God dwells with man.

The size of our gatherings won't matter. The number and success of our programs will not matter. They will know we are Christians by our love; the transforming love that come from a life in union with God.

~ ~ ~

The Jesus Prayer is the Pearl of Great Price that emerged from the heart of the desert. Countless Neptic Fathers and Hesychasts wrote number-less texts on the prayer and its practice. There is no end to information on the prayer. This prayer is also a part of our diet.

The prayer is simple, but endless in its depth:

Lord Jesus Christ . . .

Son of God . . .

Have mercy on me . . .

A sinner.

I have saved this prayer until the end, because in all of our am-blings around cairn-space and the sacramental life we are really only at the beginning of our journey in Jesus. There is no greater practice than the Jesus Prayer. It is the greatest bridge into the silent stillness of the Presence. Other practices prepare us for this gift. For this prayer we should sell all we have to buy the field within which it is hidden.

This prayer is often accompanied with a slow and steady attention to the beating of the heart and our breathing. Many pass the knots of the "komboschini" (prayer rope) through their fingers as they pray the prayer. The prayer is prayed slowly and with attention to the heart. We watch what arises, acknowledge it and pick up the prayer again.

The most ideal setting for the prayer is to sit, eyes closed and pray the prayer. We should remain imageless in our thoughts and impres-sions (according to Evagrios). This is why we have waited until now to speak of the prayer.

We must have some mastery of sitting in imagelessness while pray-ing before we begin this prayer. Arisings will occur, but we will not force our own images onto our practice of this prayer. We will not imagine sitting with Jesus or any other visualization when in the most refined practice of the prayer. We acknowledge the arisings and develop our new pathways with the prayer alone.

This is a practice for the Church as well as the individual. It is gem for corporate and solitary practice because it is so simple. When incorporating the practice of the Jesus Prayer into communal settings it is helpful to read from the writings of the Neptic Fathers on the topic. Direction will come from the "words" the Fathers have to offer.

If there is to be union and hope for the community of the Church and for the individual believer we know it will and must be in Jesus. The prayer provides a beautiful place to begin the long journey home.

The Jesus prayer takes us into the heart—the place of union with God. The heart is the place of meeting. Go there and wander. The heart is the eye of the storm.

We need to have a set of resources to feed ourselves and our communities on. There needs to be a collection of manuscripts and books, websites and newsletters. We should plug into "listening posts" that will build our ability to build our interior. I would recommend:

- The Apophthegmata Patrum—"Sayings of the Fathers"
- Thomas Merton's works on prayer and contemplation
- "Merton and Hesychasm: The Prayer of the Heart and the Eastern Church," Fons Vitae Press
- "The Philokalia", Faber and Faber
- Father Anthony DeMello's works
- "The Jesus Prayer: The Ancient Desert Prayer that Tunes the Heart to God," Fredrica Matthewes-Greene
- Father Thomas Keatings works
- Father Basil Pennington's works
- Father Teilhard de Chardin's works

"A brother in Scetis went to ask for a word from Abba Moses and the old man said to him, "Go and sit in your cell and your cell will teach you everything.""

—THE SAYINGS OF THE DESERT FATHERS

Abba Anthony said: "The time is coming when people will be seized by manias and will behave like madmen. And if they see anyone acting reasonably, they will rise up against him saying: 'You are insane.' And they will have accurately said this to him, for he will not be like them."

—The Sayings of the Desert Fathers

"Opposed to the idea that the world of perception is the bottom of reality, the mystics plunge into what is beneath the perceptible. What they attain in their quest is more than a vague impression or spotty knowledge of the imperceptible. "Penetrating to the real essence of wisdom . . . they are resplendent with the radiance of supernal wisdom (Zohar II)." Their eyes perceive things of this world, while their hearts reverberate to the throbbing of the hidden."

—Rabbi Abraham Joshua Heschel
The Mystical Element in Judaism